Praise for *A Complicated Choice*

"A critical, essential offering to the national conversation about abortion that invites us to listen to those most impacted: the people who have made these decisions themselves. *A Complicated Choice* is a truly important offering for the United States today."

—Rabbi Danya Ruttenberg, author of *Surprised by God* and *Nurture the Wow*; Scholar in Residence, National Council of Jewish Women

"Katey Zeh creates conditions for choice and agency to guide the path for healing and community for those who walk the path of abortion."

—Robyn Henderson-Espinoza, PhD, author of *Body Becoming* and *Activist Theology*

"Katey Zeh takes on concepts of stigma and privilege without demur. She brings a powerful perspective as a woman of faith, and relies on that faith to open a fulsome and compassionate dialogue with people about their individual experiences with abortion in a series of interviews."

—Herminia Palacio, president and CEO of the Guttmacher Institute

"Sharing personal stories, coupled with a fresh perspective on some well-known gospel verses, Katey Zeh brings so much compassion and nuance to the conversation about abortion."

—Asha Dahya, author of *Today's Wonder Women: Everyday Superheroes Who Are Changing the World*

"In spaces where there is so much yelling and screaming about abortion, Rev. Zeh has taken the time to slow the pace, to listen and share, to shape a healing process that doesn't include blame or shame."

—Pastor Kaji Dousa, senior pastor, Park Avenue Christian Church

"Refreshingly relatable. Zeh gifts her audience with concrete ways to wrestle with faith and abortion, making this book a significant resource for religious and medical communities as well as public policy influencers."

—Monique Moultrie, associate professor of religious studies and director of undergraduate studies, Georgia State University

A COMPLICATED CHOICE

A COMPLICATED CHOICE

MAKING SPACE FOR GRIEF AND HEALING IN THE PRO-CHOICE MOVEMENT

KATEY ZEH

FOREWORD BY ALEXIS McGILL JOHNSON,
PRESIDENT AND CEO OF PLANNED PARENTHOOD FEDERATION OF AMERICA

BROADLEAF BOOKS
MINNEAPOLIS

For all who hold untold stories in their hearts

CONTENTS

CONTENTS

FOREWORD

COVID-19 taught all of us what isolation can do. It destabilizes our communities and tests our spirits. People who tried to access abortion during the early days of the pandemic felt this isolation acutely. As governors used the crisis as an excuse to ban abortion, some patients drove sixteen hours from Texas to California and Colorado just to access medication abortion. I think about how they must have felt on those long, lonely drives: isolated from loved ones by the virus. Isolated from their trusted providers by politicians. Terrified and utterly alone.

That wasn't by accident. To borrow from Adam Serwer: the cruelty is the point. For decades, opponents of abortion have created barriers designed to alienate patients.

Stigma, too, is meant to isolate us—and no medical procedure is more stigmatized than abortion. The truth is, abortion is common. Nearly one in four women will access it in her lifetime. But that's not the story we've been told.

Because stigma is one of the most powerful tools of oppression—it operates invisibly. It creates its own pathway in our minds and becomes difficult to overcome. It's the foundation of *the* narratives we've consumed our whole lives, so it provides a ready justification for laws that limit our freedoms. And because stigma is so pervasive, it's not just perpetuated by our opponents. When we shy away from the more complicated and nuanced side of abortion stories, intentionally or not, we isolate one another. Even our most vocal supporters have internalized false narratives about abortion, race, gender, and class. I certainly have. To unlearn these stereotypes, accumulated over a lifetime of exposure, takes real work. For as long as I've been a part of the movement for reproductive rights, I've also been exploring questions about bias. I can't untangle the two. The same decade I first volunteered for Planned Parenthood, I was also leading the Perception Institute, a consortium of researchers, advocates, and strategists. We translated mind science research into solutions that reduce bias and discrimination. I've spent the better part of my career exploring how our brains process challenging conversations and experiences.

Here's what I've learned: our brains are amazing, but they're lazy. They slip into strong archetypes that reinforce stigma, without us even realizing it's happening. But our brains also love stories. They're hard-wired to use narratives to make meaning. We can use what we know about the mind sciences to our advantage. When we share abortion stories, we're actually building new, strong archetypes against stigma. Through the seventeen stories in this book, Katey Zeh is giving us the tools to build a new practice: to, as she says, "develop our individual and collective capacity to offer compassion to one another."

Sharing a story you've been told to hide is a radical act of defiance. And choosing to witness that story—without judgment or prejudice—is a radical act of grace. In the space between the telling and the hearing, the spirit is at work. As a movement for reproductive freedom, we need to create the conditions for these radical exchanges. We need to create a space where people can be vulnerable. Where they will be seen, and accepted, for who they truly are. The seventeen storytellers in this collection have trusted Katey with their truth, and in turn, she's modeling how we can build a movement for reproductive freedom with trust as its cornerstone. Where there is room for every story in all its fullness. Where there is room for joy and ambivalence, for grief and its half-lives, for innocence and experience, for hardship and privilege. Where there is room for everyone who has had an abortion: women, men, trans and nonbinary people. Where you are not just welcome, you belong.

As the nation's leading provider of sexual and reproductive health care, Planned Parenthood has a role to play here. In our hearts and in our movements, we need to make room for all kinds of complicated, beautiful stories. We need to show people it's okay to complicate the narrative. When you share your "imperfect" abortion story, you don't hurt our cause. You actually strengthen it.

To wrestle with stories that make us uncomfortable, or bump up against our deeply ingrained stigmas, we need to be braver. We cannot be afraid—even when our fear is coming from a very logical place. As abortion advocates, we know how our words can be twisted. We're so scared to get things wrong because millions of people have trusted us to get it right. Their ability to access health care depends on it.

But life doesn't always make narrative sense. It's complicated. So are our stories.

My own faith story is complicated. Maybe yours is too. For me, there was no moment on the road to Damascus. My relationship with God didn't come easy. Like many, I rebelled against my upbringing in a characteristically cliche way: "I don't *do* organized religion. I'm more of a *spiritual* person." My mom, faith warrior that she is, would shout after me "Remember Jeremiah 29:11: 'For I know the plans I have for you, plans to prosper you and not harm you, plans to give you hope and a future.'" I envied my mom's surety in that plan during many dark times in my life, which in itself misses the point: faith emerges most clearly in dark times. It may seem ironic, but that insight is what helped me find a way into a pew to build my practice and reconcile the intangible. God speaks when we sit still and listen.

That's something Reverend Katey Zeh does so brilliantly. She listens, then brings stories to life in all their glorious, messy complexities. Her voice is as vibrant on the page as it is in our movement: unapologetic, brimming with love, and guided by faith. She has a singular talent for making us think twice about scripture we thought we knew by heart, only to find something new and transformative. She uses the Bible to hold up a mirror to the fight for gender justice today, both in these pages and in *Women Rise Up: Sacred Stories of Resistance For Today's Revolution.*

However this book found its way to you, I hope you read it with the same spirit in which Katey wrote. Bring an open heart. Give these stories permission to change you. When strong feelings surface, honor them and name them. Remember that testimonies of grief and ambivalence don't harm our fight for freedom: they *are* freedom in action. Have faith in that power.

Faith and fear cannot coexist. We always have a choice. In Mark 5:25–34, the hemorrhaging woman's faith overcame her fear. She cast off the shroud of stigma and spoke her truth. Katey Zeh asks us to consider this moment as not just healing for her—but perhaps, for everyone who witnessed her. Toni Morrison said, "The function of freedom is to free someone else." Sharing your story doesn't just free you: it gives others the tools to imagine freedom.

So step out of your fear. Tell the story on your heart—the one only you can tell.

Let's get free.

—Alexis McGill Johnson, President and CEO of
Planned Parenthood Federation of America

PREFACE

On a steamy June morning in 2007, I made the one-mile drive from my apartment to the abortion clinic where I'd scheduled my appointment. As I turned off the main road and onto the side street where the facility was located, I felt a prickling surge of adrenaline course through my body like an alarm system that had been triggered. Just outside the clinic entrance, a group of protesters, all of them gray-headed and white-presenting, took up most of the length of the sidewalk. One was an older man who wore a clerical collar and held up a Bible in his right hand. They were holding signs bearing gruesome, bloody images and condemning words in bold block lettering I did my best to ignore.

Approaching the parking lot, I had no choice but to bring my car to a near stop as I pulled up into the steep driveway. That momentary pause in my speed was their opportunity, one they had practiced and perfected. Two of the protesters approached my car, thrusting their hands toward the driver's side window, only a thin pane of glass separating us. They held pamphlets too small for me to read, but I didn't need to see them to know exactly what they said. *You don't have to kill your baby.* I kept my focus on the road, averted my eyes from theirs, and parked as far away from the sidewalk as possible.

I'd arrived at the clinic with time to spare. I'm habitually early, especially when nervous. My appointment wasn't for a few more minutes, and I wanted the chance to collect myself. I didn't want the people on the sidewalk to see just how shaken I felt. I dabbed at the beads of sweat on my forehead and estimated how long I thought the walk to the clinic entrance would take me. *OK,* I thought to myself. *This will take less than ten seconds. I can do anything for ten seconds. Then I will be inside, and I won't have to see them again until I leave.* I closed my eyes, took a deep breath, and prayed for peace. Then I stepped out of my car.

With my gaze toward the ground, I hurried across the pavement to the locked clinic door and buzzed the front desk to let them know I was there. After giving them my name, I waited a few seconds, though it felt like minutes, before being let in. That was when I realized that the group of protesters had begun screaming at me from the sidewalk. Their vicious shouts carried as I made my way inside.

"God doesn't want you to kill your baby!"

"You'll regret your abortion!"

"You don't have to do this. We can help you!"

Not that it mattered, but what the protesters didn't know was that I was not at the clinic to get an abortion that day. I was there to help care for the people who were.

While I am not among the one in four US women who has needed an abortion in her lifetime, I recognize that I could be. I've used emergency contraception. I've had late periods. I've feared that my birth control method had failed. I've prayed for a pregnancy test to be negative, and as I've waited, I've had racing thoughts about what I would do if that pink line appeared. I always imagined that I would become a parent one day, but not when I was a full-time student living with roommates, or while I was working an entry-level job that barely covered my monthly rent and student loan payments, or in the midst of leaving an unstable relationship with an emotionally absent and unemployed partner. To my great relief, the only time that a pink line appeared on a test was when I hoped and prayed it would.

When I walked into the clinic that day, I had thought about what I would encounter inside, but I had not prepared for what it would feel like to be on the *outside* as a target of the protesters' rage and shame tactics. I felt all alone, vulnerable, and completely exposed, and yet what I experienced was only a small fraction of the relentless and cruel harassment, shame, and stigma that people face every day as they try to access critical reproductive health care. That experience was jarring, not only because I had been yelled at, but also because I'd been mistaken for an abortion patient. Part of me wanted to scream back, *But I'm not here to have an abortion! I'm not even pregnant.* The fact that I cared about what these people thought of me and my reason for being there gave me pause.

Until that moment I might have felt firm in my staunchly pro-choice convictions, but being perceived as someone in need of an abortion was deeply unsettling, and I needed to unpack exactly why. In retrospect, I can see clearly that despite my beliefs that abortion should be legal and accessible, I also held a lot of judgmental views and internalized stigma about who actually gets them. In that way, I wasn't all that different from the protesters. Sure, I supported abortion in the abstract sense as a political and moral issue, but I also bought into false narratives about the people who decide to end their pregnancies—and they were not people like me. I had fallen into the trap of a common narrative shaped by patriarchy and white supremacy that while abortion should be available for others, it was not for people like me. I was convinced that I would never have one myself because I was white and middle class and had access to education.

Thanks to a whole host of unearned privileges, including affordable health care, economic resources, and a bit of good luck, I have not been in the position of making a difficult decision about a pregnancy, but I easily could have been. Had I been confronted with an unplanned pregnancy, I would have had every tool and resource available to make the best decision at the time. Tragically, that is not true for everyone—not even close. Racism, sexism, classism, ableism, xenophobia, and all other forms of oppression perpetuate systems of reproductive injustice that not only deny marginalized people access to abortion care but also deny their basic human dignity and freedom.

The summer I spent volunteering in an abortion clinic was transformative for me. Since that morning when I first entered the clinic doors, I have had the enormous honor of walking alongside many people through their reproductive journeys. While I never expected to receive a call to ministry inside that clinic, I am grateful each day that I did.

On my first day of volunteering, I was set up to shadow the clinic staff as they guided patients through the entire abortion process from intake to being discharged. I was sitting in a small office with the first patient who had agreed to let me observe her appointment. The staff member had to leave the room for a moment to get a form, and I decided to strike up a conversation with her. We had a lot in common. We were roughly the same age, both full-time students (I was studying theology and she was a criminal justice major), and in serious relationships with boyfriends we were crazy about. But of course, there was one obvious difference: she was pregnant, and I was not. I accompanied her first to her ultrasound, then to the waiting area where she changed into a medical gown, and finally to the procedure room. Patients had the option to have twilight anesthesia, a mild sedative, but she had decided against it. She had come to the clinic alone and had to drive herself home. I wondered why her boyfriend wasn't there, but I didn't pry.

As the doctor began the procedure, two tears formed at the corners of her eyes, but she did not make a sound. It sounds cliché to say, but it felt like what was happening to her body was happening to mine too. My face began to flush, my breathing got more shallow, and I broke into a sweat. Much to my embarrassment, one of the nurses had to find me a place to sit down while she fanned me with a file folder so that I wouldn't pass out. It didn't help that she was visibly annoyed while doing this. Eventually, my body calmed down, and after a quick mea culpa to the nurse, I walked over to the recovery room to check on the patient whom I'd befriended. To my astonishment, when I walked in the door, she asked me with concern in her eyes, "Are you OK?" before I could ask her the same thing. Her compassion for me, this brand-new volunteer who was clearly green around the ears, was remarkable. At the same time, she shouldn't have had to care for me in that moment. Looking back, I think my reaction was a combination of my lifelong phobia of doctors, my tendency to feel others' pain, and if I'm honest, some discomfort I had with the reality of abortion.

The week after my first volunteer shift, I attended a clinic training to learn more about the mechanics of abortion procedures and work through my own feelings about it so that the next time I was with a patient, I was equipped and prepared to center their needs, not my own. I spent most of my weekly shifts holding the hands of patients through their abortions and helping them make their way to the recovery room afterward. It was awkward and holy at the same time, being invited into these vulnerable few minutes of a person's life. One patient, a woman in her midthirties, had to return to the clinic after her medication abortion had failed to remove all of the fetal tissue from her uterus. As I helped her onto the table and offered her my hand, she locked her eyes on mine and asked me, "Could I look at you until it's over?" I saw that what I had to offer were not the perfect words of comfort or reassurance but my steadfast presence. It was profoundly simple. In those short, intense minutes, I was fully available to care for her. *This is what ministry is*, I thought to myself.

I encountered so many different kinds of people in the clinic: teenagers, women in their forties, mothers, students, Black women, Latinx women, white women, those who were fearful, those who were relieved, first-time patients and returning patients, and all of the clinic staff who cared for them with compassion and without judgment. Meanwhile, I was confronting my own biases as I came face-to-face with the realities of people's lives that my privilege and access had shielded me from.

I remember when one patient asked if she could have a copy of her ultrasound photo because she wanted to add it to her child's baby book. It wasn't my place to ask her why, but there are so many reasons she would've wanted to memorialize this lost pregnancy alongside the milestones of her child. Perhaps she had miscarried an earlier wanted pregnancy. What I didn't understand at the time was that for some people, the experience of abortion is a significant reproductive event that they need to process, grieve, and integrate into the larger story of their lives.

Each person I met that summer and every story I have heard since calls me toward greater compassion for those who access abortion care and urges me to confront the systemic injustices that prevent people from truly flourishing and experiencing the lives of abundance that Christ intends for every single person. Bearing witness to these moments and stories has freed me from trying to prove that I am "right" in the public abortion debate. I am no longer interested in circular conversations regarding the moral absolutes of abortion. What I am fully invested in is working to dismantle abortion stigma within myself, in the church, and in the world so that we can start showing up fully and lovingly for the people in our communities who have abortions.

As abortion storyteller and activist Renee Bracey Sherman says, "Everyone loves someone who had an abortion." We just don't always know it. This book will introduce you to some amazing people willing to share their abortion stories. I ask that you receive them with open hearts and abundant love.

ABOUT THE PROCESS

Abortion is never abstract. Every single one happens within a person's real, full, and complex life.

When the inspiration for this project came to me, I knew that my ability to write it hinged on the willingness and generosity of others, many of them strangers, to share their abortion experiences with me. To put it plainly, without their stories, this book would not exist. For them to trust me to listen and capture their experiences accurately and holistically was an act of faith and a precious gift that I did not accept lightly. I owe a debt of gratitude to each and every one of them for their open hearts, their authenticity, and their graciousness with me. I pray that I have done their stories justice.

At the beginning of the process, I had to determine the best way to invite people into the project. Some suggested an open call on social media, but I worried that casting the net that widely would attract people more interested in thwarting my project than supporting it. Instead, I started by testing the waters with friends who had shared their abortion stories with me in the past to see if they might be interested in participating. Every single person I contacted wanted to have their stories included, and some of them helped put me in touch with others who had stories they wanted to tell. As with any project, the word began to spiral outward, and I started to connect with people outside of my immediate circle. I want to express my deep gratitude to Sonja Spoo, Elaina Ramsey, Rabbi Danya Ruttenberg, Renee Bracey

Sherman, Beth Vial, Tatiana Perkins, and Rev. Susan Chorley for helping to shape my approach to storytelling in ways that center the storytellers and for connecting me with many of the people included in this book.

Over the course of the summer of 2020, I conducted a total of nineteen interviews. Given that we were in the middle of the COVID-19 pandemic, all of the interviews were done via phone or videoconference, oftentimes with my then five-year-old daughter darting into the room every few minutes. To put it mildly, the conditions were not ideal for this kind of intimate conversation. Dropped signals, spotty internet connections, and frozen screens were frequent interruptions. In a perfect world, I would have been able to meet these extraordinary people in person and share a cup of coffee or tea while we talked. On the other hand, connecting virtually was at times helpful. It allowed for more privacy and discretion, which helped some interviewees feel more comfortable disclosing certain details.

Before sharing their stories individually, I want to highlight the various backgrounds and identities of the storytellers. Their ages range from late teens to midsixties. They live in nearly every region of the country, some from states with the most restrictive abortion legislation and others from states with the most access. They identify as white, Black, Asian, and Latinx. They are straight and queer, cisgender and transgender, abled and disabled, parents and people without children, partnered and single, living in poverty and living with financial means. They are Christian, Jewish, formerly evangelical, spiritual, and atheist.

I began each interview the same way, by introducing the project, explaining why I was doing it, and asking the person about what their healing process surrounding abortion has looked like. From there, I let the conversation expand organically and asked clarifying questions. Some people were ready to share their entire stories, beginning to end, without much prompting from me—almost like they just needed to get it out as quickly as possible. Other conversations were slower in their unfurling. Each person was free to share as much or as little about their experiences as they wanted to. I tried to interject as little as possible, though I'll admit that is not my strongest trait, especially when I feel inspired by what someone has shared! The more I spoke with different people, the more I began to see the threads of connection among their stories. As they shared, I typed as much of their answers as I could in real time and afterward returned to the recording, which each person consented to, to fill in any gaps. Several of the people I interviewed contacted me after our conversation to share things that they had forgotten. Some sent me blog posts, articles, and poetry that they had written about their abortions, which I tried to incorporate into my retelling of their stories whenever possible.

After completing all of the interviews, I crafted a first draft of each story, printed them off, and began to meditate on them. Truly, the stories showed me the way forward. At first, organizing them under common themes was an overwhelming process because so many patterns and similarities showed up in story after story. After some shuffling, I began to weave sets of narratives together in my mind and settled on a single frame for each grouping. Then I began to do my research of how these particular stories pointed to underlying systemic issues, oftentimes matters of social inequity but also concepts of how we collectively make sense of things that happen in our lives. My research assistant, Rose Miller, was a tremendous help to me during this portion of the process. She dutifully looked up journal articles, read books, and took copious notes, quickly shifting gears as I refined my project time and time again. Once I had a first draft of their stories, I contacted each of the interviewees to provide feedback, critique, and corrections. Two of them decided in the end not to have their stories included. Each of the seventeen storytellers whose stories appear in the book has given their approval.

Looking back, nineteen interviews is both a lot and not much at all. The accounts in this book in no way represent every single kind of abortion story. I know some particular experiences are missing: the experiences of Indigenous people, undocumented immigrants, trans men, and those who had abortions in the third trimester. I recognize that this is in part because of my own distance from these communities and the additional stigma and barriers that people in these groups experience in telling their abortion stories.

Recognizing the very real limits of this project, I do hope that the stories included will shift the ways that we approach conversations about abortion both privately and publicly and especially in Christian circles. I hope that I can leverage my privilege as a white, straight woman and an ordained Baptist minister to amplify the experiences of those most impacted by the culture of shame and stigma surrounding abortion—and that their wisdom would shape our responses to abortion moving forward.

A NOTE ON LANGUAGE

Access to abortion is a matter of human rights that impacts all of us, regardless of our gender identity. Throughout the book, I use gender-inclusive terms like *pregnant people* and *people who can become pregnant*. This is to ensure that the language is inclusive of people who have abortions who do not identify as cisgender women, including trans men and nonbinary individuals, as well as to acknowledge that not all cisgender women are capable of becoming pregnant. Recognizing that language is ever evolving, in our pursuit of reproductive freedom and dignity for all people, let us commit to using the terms, language, and frames that hold space for all of us.

PART 1

INTRODUCTION

1

HONORING YOUR EXPERIENCE OF ABORTION

But the woman, knowing what had happened to her, came in fear
and trembling, fell down before him, and told him the whole truth.

—Mark 5:33

One of my favorite Bible stories is in the Gospel of Mark. A woman
has been suffering from hemorrhaging for twelve years. Her constant
bleeding destroys her strength and presumably her fertility. In her
search for a cure, she spends all of the money she has on doctors who
offer her no relief and only make her worse. This alone is a tragedy. But
beyond her physical suffering, the stigma associated with her personal
health crisis leaves her socially isolated. The rules and norms of her
society dictate where a bleeding woman is permitted to go and what

kind of social relationships she is allowed to have. For over a decade, her suffering has been a source of great oppression, defining the boundaries of her life and her identity in the eyes of others. Even the writer of the Gospel refers to her only by her condition, not her name.

When the woman learns that a healer named Jesus will be coming through her town, she realizes that this may be her last chance to save her own life. It is time for her to abandon the societal rules that have failed her, to stop asking for permission to heal, and to risk taking what she needs. When Jesus passes her in a crowd, she reaches out to touch his clothing, her fingers barely grazing the bottom hem of his garment. She feels the shift in her body instantly. Her bleeding has stopped. But that is only the beginning of her healing.

Jesus stops in his tracks and asks the crowd, "Who touched me?" The woman, having been healed, could have decided to leave unnoticed. But she feels drawn to the possibility of something even more miraculous: liberation. Despite her fear, this cured woman chooses to tell Jesus, as the story says, the *whole* truth. I imagine that telling her story and recounting the details of her suffering is gut-wrenching. But as she breaks the silence of her years of isolation and gives voice to her pain, she finds full and complete healing.

This woman's display of courage to proclaim her truth in front of Jesus is more than a personal healing story. Jesus is not the only one who hears her speak. In the crowd surrounding the healer and the healed one are people who have shunned this woman for her bleeding and blamed her for her suffering. They are the ones who have been complicit in her oppression. I wonder, What impact does her story have on them? How might her truth serve as a catalyst for social change?

I also imagine that among the people gathered around Jesus and the woman are those who long for their own healing. They, too, live with secret struggles and pain. Who else might be healed by her courage to end the silence and speak her truth?

After hearing her story, Jesus responds with compassion and kindness. He doesn't ask what caused her bleeding to begin with. He doesn't blame or shame her. He calls her daughter and says that her faith has made her well. Her faith to go against the cultural rules that kept her sick and oppressed. Her faith to seek her own healing without asking for permission. Her faith to overcome her fear and to share her story, no matter the cost.

What if it was her willingness to reach out not only her hand but also her heart that healed her?

In the Gospel of John, Jesus says to his disciples, "The truth will set you free" (8:32). Truth-telling frees all of us, but it takes faith, strength, and bravery. Embracing our inner knowing requires us first to shed the stories others have given us that have silenced and shamed us from speaking up and speaking out.

Like the unhelpful experts who took advantage of the hemorrhaging woman's vulnerability, others can be far too eager to offer help that actually hurts us. They draw uninformed conclusions and take it upon themselves to define what is right and wrong for everyone else. Without understanding or acknowledging our personal circumstances, they insist on a truth they claim is absolute, offering simple answers to life's complex questions. They wield these tools of oppression, disguised in the language of love and helpfulness, at our most vulnerable moments. Whether their intentions are to harm or to heal, they push us deeper into isolation instead of toward liberation.

This is true for many of the sacred decisions we make about our bodies, families, and futures. It is especially true for the decision to have an abortion. Everyone claims to have the "right" answer about what someone else ought to do when faced with a pregnancy they cannot continue. We hear the angry protester who stands outside the abortion clinic and shouts words of condemnation. We witness the white conservative male politician as he cites pseudoscience and the Bible to introduce restrictive abortion legislation while denying Medicaid expansion, ignoring rising rates of maternal mortality among Black women, and refusing to pass truly life-giving policies. We have the friend, or the partner, or the family member who lacks the compassionate words and the willingness to listen with an open mind and heart. We recall the early messages from faith leaders and family members about sex, sin, and worthiness in the eyes of God. They say to us, "You are a sinner, and you cannot trust yourself to know what is best for your life."

Thankfully, the Gospel story offers us a different path to claim our inner knowing that comes in the quiet stillness of our hearts. This account of a woman's healing of body, mind, and spirit is a testament to the truth that so many times, we know exactly what we need. We have the power to be the catalyst for our own healing and flourishing. Though others may try to sway us to make different choices, the divine voice of God is always there within us, whispering words of truth, nudging us toward the best path for our circumstances, and reminding us that we are never alone. If we can tune out the voices that condemn, judge, and make false promises of healing, we can begin to recognize the sound of sacred wisdom that speaks to us with love and truth:

You are a child of God.
Your faith will make you well.
Your truth will set you free.

If you are among the millions of people who have ended pregnancies, I hope that this book serves as an encouragement and a guide for honoring the truth of your journey, for finding the healing you need, and for working toward the healing of our world. Whether you are making a decision about a pregnancy now or reflecting on a decision you made in the past, whether you felt like you had a real choice or not, whether your path was clear or complicated, whether you had support or not, whether you feel relief or grief (or both), your story is sacred, and it belongs to you. As you encounter others' experiences, even those seemingly different from yours, I pray that you feel a sense of connection to this community of people who have abortions. I hope you feel seen, heard, and affirmed.

How you feel about your reproductive decisions, talk about them, and process them is all part of your healing journey. As you read the stories within this book, a number of emotions may arise for you: sadness, anger, resentment, despair, loneliness, hope, joy, relief, and more. No emotion is wrong or bad to experience, even if the feeling is unpleasant. But we suffer unnecessarily when we refuse to acknowledge our true feelings about a situation or when we bury them deep within ourselves, only to find them triggered later.

These feelings may be uncomfortable or even painful to endure, but they are not an indication that you made the wrong decision to end the pregnancy. Asking yourself what might have been if you had taken a different path is a normal part of making a decision about your life. When these doubts or questions arise, try to view them as an opportunity to show yourself more compassion and love—and to receive love from others.

If you feel grief or a sense of loss about any aspect of your abortion journey, I want you to know that your pain is not a punishment from God. If there is one thing of which I am certain about God, it's that God is with you in your pain and your journey to healing. Sometimes I imagine Jesus walking by an abortion clinic. He does not join the protesters on the sidewalk. He does not keep walking by. He accompanies patients so that they don't have to go into the clinic alone. He speaks words of reassurance as he holds their hands. He gives them a paper cup of ginger ale and a saltine in the recovery room. He offers his loving, compassionate presence throughout it all.

Abortion is a deeply personal experience. Every pregnant person who decides to have an abortion does so within a unique set of life circumstances and realities that only they can understand completely. At the same time, threads of connection exist between your personal experience and the lives of many other people for whom abortion is part of their reproductive journeys. As you honor the truth of your personal story, I invite you, if you haven't already, to reflect on how your experience is intertwined within a larger human story of reproductive injustice and oppression, the roots of which are ancient and deep and are entangled with racism, sexism, heterosexism, classism, ableism, and other systems of oppression.

Some of these connections might be apparent to you, while others may be less obvious. If you are a person with privilege of any kind, it may require some deep and hard work as you examine your ability or inability to make certain reproductive choices. If you identify as white, it will mean thinking about white supremacy and how that shapes your access to care. If you have economic resources, it will mean thinking about how the cost of abortion was not a barrier to your access. If you accessed abortion care in a state without cumbersome legal restrictions, I invite you to reflect on what it would have been like to face these obstacles. Many factors shape our reproductive journey, and understanding our own helps us deepen our compassion for others who face different challenges and obstacles.

In facing this deep systemic oppression that impacts the ways we are able to move through the world in our bodies, we may feel overwhelmed, but we find ways to hold onto hope. As people of faith, we share a common belief in that which is unseen and greater than any one of us. Together we dare to imagine a world we believe is possible, a thriving society rooted in the values of freedom, dignity, and compassion so that every person, family, and community flourishes fully. We turn our collective pain into a force of loving power that propels us forward in our faithful pursuit of a more just, compassionate world for all.

Healing our world and healing ourselves are one and the same. Just as there are many experiences of abortion, there are many pathways to healing and wholeness. This book will offer many different stories of people's abortions, their emotional journeys, and their ways of moving forward in their lives as more compassionate, caring, and nonjudgmental people. As you read their stories, release any expectations of what your process should look like and embrace whatever unfolds, knowing that there is no wrong way to be on this journey and that God is with you always. Ask yourself, What is the truth about my abortion experience and my life that would set me free? What am

I willing to risk for my freedom? How might embracing and owning my truth help to free others?

As a minister and an advocate for reproductive freedom and dignity, I pray that this book is a balm for your soul and that as you find healing and love for yourself, these stories help guide us all toward the path of our collective liberation.

May we all be set free.

2

UNCOVERING THE CULTURE OF SHAME, STIGMA, AND SILENCE AROUND ABORTION

As I shared in the preface, I do not have a personal abortion story. I once thought this was a detriment. How could I advocate effectively for something I had not experienced personally?

We don't need to experience something personally to care for those who do. I may never understand fully what it's like to end a pregnancy, but I can choose to respond with compassion when someone shares their abortion story with me.

When I talk about compassion, I'm careful not to conflate it with empathy. While empathy involves feeling someone else's experience as our own, which can be overwhelming and even numbing, compassion is a process that moves us into taking action that centers the one in need. *Compassion is active.* All of us can learn to be more compassionate, but doing so requires self-awareness, reflection, and regular practice.

Until my midtwenties, I didn't know anyone in my life who'd had an abortion because no one told me. If no one has told you about their abortion, I can assure you there are people in your community, your circle of friends, and most likely your family who have ended pregnancies.

Imagine that someone you love told you they needed an abortion. How do you think you would respond? What feelings might come up for you? If someone has come to you in the past about a decision to end a pregnancy, what was that experience like? If you could do it over again, what would you do differently?

Talking about abortion can be incredibly difficult. It makes sense that we might choose to opt out because we're uncomfortable and don't know what to think or say. Being honest about where we are on our journey and showing ourselves grace are part of becoming more compassionate, because we have to be kind to ourselves if we hope to grow in kindness toward others.

In college, I wrote my senior honors thesis on a theology of motherhood. During my defense, one of my committee members asked if I had considered addressing abortion. In the wrong hands, she warned, my text could be weaponized against legal abortion. I grew quiet. I hadn't mentioned abortion because I honestly hadn't seen the relevance to my work. (This is a time when I have to show my younger self compassion for my naïveté.) I didn't see how interconnected abortion and parenthood were at the time.

Perhaps you can relate. Many Christians I know, especially those who identify as white and progressive, say they support legal abortion, but they have a hard time affirming it as a morally sound choice. *I would never have an abortion, but I think other people should be able to do what is right for them* is a common sentiment expressed by politically pro-choice people. As Christian ethicist Rebecca Todd Peters writes in her book *Trust Women: A Progressive Christian Argument for Reproductive Justice*, many of us believe that abortion is only OK for other people, not for us.

When we keep quiet about abortion, or when our support is lukewarm and detached, we signal to people that we would rather not hear about their experiences. There is a culture of silence around abortion, and that silence is shaming and isolating on both a personal and a collective level. We have to face our internalized abortion stigma. Otherwise, we keep ourselves at arm's length from the lived reality of abortion—and from the people who need our support and compassion the most.

As Christians, we have to reckon with the fact that the antiabortion political movement draws on theological language and biblical texts in order to stigmatize people who have abortions and limit their access to reproductive health care. This extreme "pro-life" ideology is steeped in racism, classism, and sexism and does irreparable damage to the most vulnerable in our society, including people living in poverty, young people, undocumented people, LGBTQ+ people, and people of color.

We have an opportunity and a responsibility to call out this harm and begin to repair it. This work will be uncomfortable, even painful, as we acknowledge the ways we have failed and have been complicit in these unjust systems and practices, but in coming together, we take active, purposeful steps toward cocreating with God a world we long to inhabit, one that supports the human flourishing of all people.

Before we can begin the work of building our compassion and healing the culture of shame surrounding abortion, we need to establish an understanding of how we ended up in this current climate. When and how did we become so polarized around this issue? When and how did Christianity writ large become synonymous with being opposed to abortion? In short, it was no accident.

Though the history of Christian views on abortion goes back centuries, for the sake of our discussion, I will focus primarily on the time period just prior to the *Roe v. Wade* Supreme Court decision and the immediate aftermath that continue to influence the public discourse on abortion today.

You may be surprised to learn that in the late 1960s and early 1970s, mainline Protestant, Jewish, and Unitarian clergy, along with laity across religious traditions, were at the forefront of the movement to legalize abortion in the United States. A robust network of faith leaders called the Clergy Consultation Service on Abortion operated throughout the country to help more than 450,000 women access safe abortion from reputable providers, even though the procedure was mostly illegal. The network also advocated publicly for the expansion of abortion rights at the state and national levels. In retrospect, these clergy may seem like radical activists on the fringes of their religious traditions. While their actions were certainly bold and courageous, they mostly had support from their governing religious bodies. Many mainline Protestant denominations spoke in support of the *Roe v. Wade* decision, as evidenced by their public statements at the time. For example, in a 1976 resolution, the Southern Baptist Convention

(SBC) affirmed their "conviction about the limited role of government in dealing with matters relating to abortion, and support[ed] the right of expectant mothers to the full range of medical services and personal counseling for the preservation of life and health."[1]

Today this piece of religious history seems all but forgotten. What happened? I spoke with scholar Dr. Gillian Frank, who shared the historical and political context of the time. In the 1960s, a time of expanding civil rights, white conservative Catholics, Mormons, and evangelicals—three religious groups that had little in common theologically but shared social interest in the submission of women and the continuation of racial segregation—began to form a political alliance to oppose legal abortion and integration. This religious voting faction was critical to the 1972 reelection of Richard Nixon, whose campaign was "fueled by racist dog whistles to white Southerners and to white urban and suburban Catholics."[2] A year later, *Roe v. Wade* made abortion legal in every state. Suddenly, abortion was no longer something hidden from view. Now it was widely available and visible, and this reality made many white, conservative-leaning voters uncomfortable. According to Frank, this is when abortion started to become a right-wing issue, especially for white voters: "When *Roe* legalized abortion, it made the process accessible to everyone, and this made some people very uneasy. For them, abortion was never decent, but it was a necessity. Once it became widely available, people who had always said abortion was wrong joined with those who were uncomfortable with abortion being a widely accessible and practiced reality in public. They were much more comfortable when abortion was invisible, hidden, and not in every community."[3] Though the religious antiabortion movement preceded the rise of the political religious right, it had gained a broadening political base and the momentum needed to dismantle the progress made for reproductive freedom and civil rights more generally. From its inception, the political antiabortion movement fueled by religious conservatives has been linked with white supremacy and Christian nationalism. For decades, its overwhelmingly white and majority male leadership has pushed a legislative agenda aimed at making abortion practically inaccessible by restricting the use of government funds for abortion care in federal health programs like Medicaid and those that serve Indigenous people living on reservations; imposing medically unnecessary restrictions on abortion providers and clinics at the state level; and implementing other obstacles, like mandatory waiting periods, parental notification laws, and bans on procedures at different stages of gestation. These laws disproportionately impact people living in poverty, young people, immigrant communities, and Black and brown communities. The messaging of the antiabortion movement, however, purports itself to be both "prowoman" and the protector of Black people from "genocide." Nowhere within their antiabortion framework is a recognition of the hundreds of years of reproductive oppression of Black women through slavery, forced sterilization, mass incarceration, and other forms of reproductive control sanctioned and practiced by the state.[4]

The well-funded, well-organized antiabortion movement sprouted branches of influence that began to permeate the dominant culture with its oppressive values of patriarchy, white supremacy, anti-Black racism, and Christian nationalism. President Ronald Reagan, backed by the religious right, waged a "war on drugs" that targeted Black communities and fueled mass incarceration while he waged another battle against the sexual health and well-being of young people by funding abstinence-only education in public schools.

At the same time, white evangelical communities, in response to the sexual revolution of the 1960s, fixated on sexual abstinence as a means of controlling the sexuality of young people, especially white women, giving rise to the "purity culture" of the 1990s. Although the principles of Christian purity culture were not new, they were now being promoted and paid for by the federal government. On a spiritual level, this rise of purity culture propped up and reinforced antiabortion ideology: that those capable of becoming pregnant cannot be trusted to make moral decisions about their bodies and that being subservient to (white, male) leadership is required to honor God.

It's not surprising, then, that one of the most influential voices in the antiabortion movement is a white conservative evangelical. David Reardon, the founder of the nonprofit Elliot Institute for Social Science Research, is one of the most outspoken proponents of the ideology that "abortion hurts women," a framing that purports to center women while stripping them of their bodily autonomy and reproductive dignity. Reardon is *not* a social scientist; he is an engineer by training. Despite his lack of credentials in any field relevant to mental health, Reardon has managed to amass a body of written works in order to produce evidence of what some antiabortion activists refer to as "postabortion syndrome," a type of post-traumatic stress resulting from an abortion. Notably, the American Psychological Association has never verified the existence of any such condition. Nevertheless, Reardon has published numerous books and articles to substantiate the prevalence of this fictitious condition. He often co-writes with psychologist and fellow antiabortion researcher Dr. Priscilla Coleman, and their published work together has had an enormous influence on the antiabortion movement.

The angle of antiabortion proponents like Reardon has been to paint their cause as an effort not only to save babies from being murdered but to save women from the trauma of abortion. Abortion, they claim, is antiwoman, and thus women deserve better than abortion. What is it exactly that would be "better"? By focusing exclusively on the aftereffects of abortion, they opt out of any and every opportunity to engage the hard work of addressing systems of oppression that result in the underlying circumstances that contribute to the decision to have an abortion: economic inequality, gender-based violence, lack of social support for parents and families, and so on. In this way, antiabortion activists have attempted to hide their ultimate purpose—to make abortion illegal—under the guise of helping women. (In reality, making abortion illegal does not stop abortion; it only makes it less safe. We need only look at data from countries where abortion is entirely or mostly illegal to see that unsafe abortion contributes to increased rates of pregnancy-related deaths and injuries.) By shifting away from calling those who have abortions "murderers" to calling them "victims" instead, antiabortion activists like Reardon seek to position themselves as the truly compassionate ones—and it's worked.

While Reardon's ultimate goal is to make abortion illegal, his insistence on the prevalence of postabortion syndrome has swayed policy makers and certain sectors of the public to believe that abortion causes high rates of mental illness and psychological disorders, which has influenced the passage of legislation that impacts abortion care.[5] In 2005, his testimony before a South Dakota legislative task force helped shape their "informed consent" abortion law, which requires providers to tell their patients that abortion increases their risk of depression and suicide, a claim that has never been proven by any reputable psychological study. This same testimony later influenced another law in South Dakota that requires providers to ask people seeking abortion care if they have been coerced into terminating their pregnancies. Along with these consent laws, Reardon has advocated for legislation that would allow patients to pursue legal action against abortion providers for any mental illness they have following their procedures.

In addition to shaping antiabortion legislation, Reardon's claims have influenced the highest levels of our judicial system. In 2007, Supreme Court Justice Anthony Kennedy, in his majority opinion to uphold an abortion ban, referred to the "severe depression and loss of esteem" that women experience because they regret their abortions, even as he admitted the lack of "reliable data to measure the phenomenon."[6] It's beyond concerning and infuriating that unsubstantiated claims about the negative emotional and psychological impacts of abortion have the power to shape the landscape of reproductive health care access in this country.

For us to understand the significance of Reardon's influence, we need to examine not only the political ramifications but also the spiritual consequences of his narratives about abortion. Reardon's motivations are at least in part religious. He has written that abortion is a sin that Satan encourages women to commit and that choosing abortion is a rejection of God's gift of a pregnancy: "Remember, your abortion was a result of your failure to trust God. In giving you that pregnancy, God was giving you the opportunity to love. But you rejected this gift because you did not trust God's plan for you."[7] His antiabortion theology and pseudoscience have inspired an overabundance of books, videos, organizations, and other resources that claim to offer healing after an abortion, but like Reardon's works, they are steeped in judgment, shame, and bad science. Much like antiabortion crisis pregnancy centers that pose as health clinics offering reproductive health services, this body of work has the appearance of helpfulness and solidarity but in reality promotes misconceptions about abortion as universally harmful to those who have them and universally sinful against God.

Many of the resources that address healing after an abortion are based on the author's personal story of abortion and grief and serve as acts of repentance. One notable example is *Her Choice to Heal: Finding Spiritual and Emotional Peace after Abortion* by Sydna Masse, founder of the antiabortion organization Ramah International, which provides resources for crisis pregnancy centers. In the book, Masse details her own abortion experience, which inspires her afterabortion ministry work now. The book is the basis of Masse's free online abortion recovery program for "postabortive individuals" and begins with an explanation of postabortion syndrome. While Masse addresses common emotions like denial, anger, and grief, she attributes them to sin that needs to be forgiven and healed by God (and with her help and resources) rather than acknowledging that these feelings are normal responses to any kind of loss and/or change in a person's life. She ends her course with tips for how to share abortion stories or "testimonies" about their sin of abortion and being forgiven by God with public audiences.

What I find fascinating and maddening is that Masse had reproductive freedom and exercised her reproductive rights in having an abortion, yet she has established a career out of telling others that they ought not have the same choices available to them. She may regret her abortion and view it as a sin, but regardless, she had access to health care when she needed it.

Abortion healing ministries like Masse's are designed in part to evangelize and recruit abortion storytellers to further the anti-abortion political agenda. Perhaps the most robust example of this is Project Rachel, a worldwide organization funded by Priests for Life and Anglicans for Life that targets people who have had abortions and their partners. Like Masse's book and course, they rely heavily on David Reardon's questionable findings to substantiate their claims about the effects of abortion on mental health to promote Rachel's Vineyard, postabortion retreats that are held worldwide. The website for Rachel's Vineyard advertises these retreats as "therapy" (though it's unclear if their retreat facilitators are licensed therapists), but in other places, they claim these retreats are a form of evangelization.[8] Certainly, these retreats have larger aims than personal healing. Rachel's Vineyard recruits attendees to participate in Silent No More, a public antiabortion advocacy campaign that is also funded by Priests for Life. The same priest who directs Rachel's Vineyard, Fr. Frank Pavone, also directs Silent No More. One of their efforts is to recruit women to stand with signs that say "I regret my abortion" at rallies and protests about abortion rights. On the Silent No More YouTube page are hundreds of public testimonies from women who attended Rachel's Vineyard retreats and are now outspoken advocates against abortion.

While I have no doubt there are some who do find healing through organizations like Project Rachel and Ramah International, I suspect many others who are vulnerable and feel they have no other place to turn are drawn in under the false promises of emotional healing and are lured into a narrative of shame and a theology of sin.

Do people actually regret their abortions as much as Silent No More's storytellers would have us believe? According to scientifically backed research, no. While some feelings of regret, guilt, and anger are common in the immediate aftermath of an abortion, the most common emotion is relief. Most people feel a combination of feelings, both positive and negative, that dissipate over time. After five years, a majority of people who have terminated pregnancies reported that they felt very few, if any, emotions surrounding their abortions.[9] While there is no credible evidence to suggest that abortion causes long-term emotional distress, that does not mean that coping with the decision to end a pregnancy is easy.

Every life decision brings an end to something. Not every ending is experienced as a loss, but often it is. Unfortunately, our society does not recognize these types of changes as losses that we grieve. Early on in my research, I came across the work of Dr. Ken Doka, a psychologist, professor, and ordained Lutheran minister. In the 1980s, Dr. Doka coined the term *disenfranchised grief* to describe losses that go against our society's "grieving rules" that dictate who and what is worthy of mourning. When we suffer a loss that we feel we cannot share with others because that loss is not recognized or supported openly, that is disenfranchised grief. Examples include grieving the death of an ex-spouse, a beloved pet, a miscarriage, or an abortion.

Dr. Doka sums up the problems with our collective responses to those who have had an abortion this way: "Many who affirm a loss may not sanction the act of abortion, whereas some who sanction the act may minimize the sense of loss."[10] The rhetoric of the mainstream reproductive rights movement, founded and largely led by white women, historically has centered around legality and individual bodily autonomy—that under the law, no one should be able to dictate what another person does with their body. This point is critical, but it is not sufficient for those called to care for people who have experienced abortion. Focusing on the point of decision alone, or the point of health care access alone, fails to address the process of grief and healing that some experience in the aftermath of making their decision, and it does not acknowledge the ways that people grow and change as a result.

I know from having spoken with many people about their abortions that they felt they could not express their feelings of sadness or grief because they feared they would be betraying the pro-choice cause. Even if they believe that their abortion was the right decision for them, they fear the ways in which their words may be used against them, that an antiabortion leader would use them as an example to say, "You see, this person really does regret their abortion!" As a result, they don't feel like they can share the fullness of their stories, which can cause a sense of social disconnection and hinder healing.

That is why I've written this book: to share stories that capture the emotional and spiritual nuances of abortion, the grief that may arise as part of the process, and the pathways to healing, which often entail processing the myriad circumstances surrounding the abortion experience.

As followers of Christ, we have an opportunity and a responsibility to bridge the divide that Dr. Doka describes in his work on disenfranchised grief and abortion. We can make space for the gray. We can learn to live in the tension of affirming that abortion is a moral decision that pregnant people are fully capable of making and also acknowledge that this decision may, though certainly not always, evoke feelings of ambivalence, sadness, loss, and grief. We can honor the full spectrum of abortion experiences and provide sacred spaces for anyone who needs supportive spiritual care along the way.

We can fully support the sacred decision-making of every person regarding their bodies, their families, and their futures while we also care deeply about how those decisions have impacts on a person's physical, mental, social, and spiritual well-being. We can affirm the decision to have an abortion while working for the conditions that would make parenting healthier, safer, and more joy filled for those who desire to parent.

We can hold space in both our faith communities and our own hearts for grief, relief, pain, healing, *and* joy after an abortion through our commitment to compassionate listening and our purposeful actions in seeking justice for those living on the margins. We can and we *must* reject the theology of shame and silence currently surrounding abortion in this culture and offer one rooted in the sacred truth that in all things, God journeys alongside us with abundant grace and unconditional love that will not let us go.

Together we can embody the love of Christ and become the healing community of support and compassion God has called us to be.

PART 2

THE STORIES

3

FOR ABUNDANT LIFE

For I will restore health to you, and your wounds I will heal, says
the Lord, because they have called you an outcast.

—Jeremiah 30:17

Sitting in a stuffy, cramped conference room, I watched silently
as a group of Christians, United Methodists specifically, debated
their denomination's stance on abortion. The room was packed with
antiabortion activists wearing matching neon-orange T-shirts. Only
elected delegates were allowed to speak in the session, but the presence of this activist group certainly made a statement. In the middle
of this discussion, one of the delegates, an older white man from the
United States, proposed an amendment to the existing language that,
if approved, would alter the denominational position to approve of
abortion only in instances when the pregnant person's physical life

was threatened. The official position at the time acknowledged the "tragic conflicts of life with life" that necessitate abortion, a carefully worded and nuanced phrase.[1] This delegate's proposal was articulated precisely and narrowly: the only circumstance in which an abortion could be morally justifiable was when death was imminent.

To my great relief, the amendment lacked the necessary support from a majority of delegates and failed in committee that year, but still, that scene haunts me. I have no doubt that future delegates will attempt again and again to modify the denomination's position until they are successful in narrowing the language to permit abortion only in cases of life endangerment. More than that, though, I'm still grappling with the bone-chilling realization that some of my Christian siblings believe that the only time a pregnant person's well-being matters is if they are facing certain death.

At the time of this denominational debate, my advocacy work focused primarily on the goal of lowering rates of maternal mortality through preventive measures like expanding voluntary access to a variety of contraceptive methods. I knew that pregnancy was a life-threatening condition for many women around the globe. The statistic at the time was that every two minutes, somewhere in the world a woman died from complications during pregnancy or childbirth. In fact, during the course of that General Conference, a delegate from Sierra Leone approached the debate floor for a point of personal privilege to request prayers for a woman who had died in childbirth earlier that day in her hometown. The stark reality of "tragic conflicts of life with life" was palpable in the room. We bowed our heads to pray for this woman who had died and for her baby who was now motherless, but what actions were we willing to take to end this needless suffering and preserve the full lives of pregnant people?

One of the guiding verses of my advocacy work is from the Gospel of John, when Jesus says, "I came that they may have life, and have it more abundantly" (10:10). We are created for more than mere survival. Abundant life is joy filled and fear-free, full of opportunity and hope, and it is just as much about the well-being of our communities as it is about the state of our individual lives. The two are intertwined. What I have learned from advocates in the reproductive justice movement is that all human beings have a fundamental right to conditions necessary for thriving as individuals, families, and communities. When a pregnancy conflicts with any aspect of a person's well-being, we ought to ask, How are we called to respond to the conditions that interfere with a person's ability to experience *abundant* life?

In 1973, the Supreme Court took on a very similar question regarding the status of a pregnant person's well-being. Most people are familiar with *Roe v. Wade*, which ruled that abortion was legal before viability under the right to privacy, but another lesser-known Supreme Court decision issued the same day was *Doe v. Bolton*. This case challenged an existing abortion law in Georgia that required before any procedure the approval of three doctors and a special committee to confirm that a pregnancy would "seriously and permanently" injure the pregnant person, or that the fetus had serious anomalies, or that the pregnancy was the result of rape or incest. The Supreme Court decision ruled that the restrictions were unconstitutional, that a person could access an abortion after viability for health reasons, and that "health" included the physical, emotional, psychological, and familial well-being of a pregnant person. This understanding of health reflected the definition adopted by the World Health Organization in 1948 that health was "a state of complete physical, mental, and social well-being" and "not merely the absence of disease or infirmity."[2]

Abortion opponents push back against this language because of how all-encompassing it is. The reality is that pregnancy and birth can lead to any number of complications that impact a person's health and well-being, and many of the experiences I share in later chapters will expound on this truth. For this chapter, I have included two stories that illustrate how pregnancy can put a person's health and well-being at risk and how access to abortion is lifesaving—in the greatest sense of the word—in these types of circumstances.

Cantor Sarah Myerson, Brooklyn, New York

> "No one has maternity leave for abortions or miscarriages, even if you have healing to do. Why do we let the system get away with it?"

"My story is going to be a little confusing," Sarah warned me. I smiled, unfazed. None of the abortion stories I'd heard had been straightforward or simple. But she was right. I hadn't yet heard a story quite as complex as hers.

Sarah had been traveling with her spouse, a professional musician, on tour throughout Europe and Canada. With the constant upheaval and numerous changes in time zones, she didn't think too much when her period was late. After returning home to the United States, they moved to their new home in Brooklyn, where Sarah started a new job. She also finally got her period, but the bleeding continued for more than a week, much longer than a typical period. On the eighth day of bleeding, while at work teaching a class, she felt something shift in her body. She rushed to the bathroom, where she had what she guessed was a miscarriage, and then returned to her classroom, trying to compartmentalize what just happened. That evening, she took a pregnancy test. It was positive.

Sarah didn't have an opportunity to seek medical care immediately. She had plans to go out of town early the next morning for a wedding. "That's what we do as clergy," she said. "We participate in these life cycle events and put ourselves last." The day she flew home, she was still bleeding, and she went straight to urgent care, wearing the same dress she'd worn to the ceremony. A blood test confirmed that she did have high levels of pregnancy hormones in her system, but the ultrasound did not detect a pregnancy. Based on the test results and her symptoms, the doctors determined that most likely she was having a miscarriage and that the bleeding would continue for some time, but it would stop eventually.

Sarah continued to bleed for weeks, and she suspected something else was going on medically. Not knowing her way around her new neighborhood in Brooklyn, she went to the hospital closest to her apartment. She was on Medicaid at the time, and the facility wasn't well resourced. Many of the patients getting treatment there had no insurance. Getting test results took longer than Sarah expected. Based on her symptoms, the doctors guessed that she might have an ectopic pregnancy, a potentially life-threatening condition in which a fertilized egg implants and grows somewhere other than in the uterus, typically inside the fallopian tube, where the embryo gets "stuck" on its way to the uterus. Ectopic pregnancies occur in about one in fifty pregnancies, and they are the main cause of first-trimester maternal deaths.[3] One of the major difficulties in treating ectopic pregnancies is that there is no way to detect that one has occurred without surgical intervention.

Before resorting to surgery, the doctors suggested a less invasive treatment first. They would inject Sarah with a low dose of chemotherapy called Methotrexate, which slows down the growth of cells and is often effective in treating most early ectopic pregnancies. "I had this fleeting thought of 'Is this an abortion?'" she said. "I would be terminating the pregnancy, which is illegal in some states. I wasn't sure if this was in alignment with Jewish law and if I should consult with someone." In the moment, though, she told herself, *This is just an injection*, and she was desperate for her bleeding to stop. She agreed to the treatment.

Her bleeding *still* didn't stop. Sarah began experiencing other symptoms that were endangering her health. She decided to seek a second opinion and scheduled an appointment with a gynecologist, who discovered that Sarah had a large cyst on her ovary that needed to be removed immediately. The doctor referred her to another hospital, one better resourced than the first she'd visited, for emergency surgery that same day. Five weeks after her bleeding began, Sarah finally got the medical care she needed to end the ectopic pregnancy that had implanted in her fallopian tube. During her operation, the surgeon also removed an ovarian cyst that was five centimeters in diameter and was near the point of rupture. In the end, they had to make six incisions in Sarah's abdomen in order to remove the cyst, the damaged fallopian tube, and part of one ovary. She had been pregnant for twelve weeks. "A fertilized egg is tiny, and a uterus is made to accommodate the growth of the embryo," she explained. "The fallopian tube is not. And it's not built to be split open and stitched up again."

Though her surgeon had talked through the possibilities of what they might find, when Sarah woke up from the procedure, she didn't know exactly what they had found. All she knew was that she was in agonizing pain from the incisions and the intubation. But she also felt an overwhelming sense of gratitude and awe for the people who had provided her medical care. She was grateful that her care was covered by her Medicaid insurance. "Otherwise, I would have gone bankrupt," she said.

She later shared with me that this entire experience illustrated to her how classism and systemic racism impact access to health care, given the stark differences between her two hospital visits: "Going to that first hospital really opened my eyes as to how low the level of care is for people who are uninsured or underinsured. It's not just luck that I had Medicaid and could go to a better hospital."

Right after the surgery, Sarah had wanted to go to the *mikve*, a ritual bath that many Jewish women visit monthly after menstruation as well as after reproductive experiences like birth, miscarriage, and abortion. Mentally and physically, however, she was not ready. After some time when she sensed she was close to having her first postsurgery period, Sarah forced herself to go. "I wanted this visit to the mikve to be different from the regular monthly purification ritual," she told me. When she got there, Sarah needed to share about her ectopic pregnancy and abortion with the mikve attendant, who responded compassionately and offered Sarah many blessings. Once Sarah entered the waters of the mikve, she described it as feeling like she was going through the abortion experience all over again. "I cried. I lost it. I kept asking 'why' questions. Why me? Why this? Why is this a necessary part of life?" she asked. "Questioning is a stage of grief, and I had questions with no answers."

After her visit to the mikve came the ritual of Yizkor, which involves lighting a candle that burns for twenty-four hours and calling to memory those who have passed. Yizkor is practiced four times throughout the religious calendar and then again on the anniversary of a loved one's death. After Sarah's abortion, the first Yizkor coincided with the week of what would have been her due date (since an ectopic pregnancy is not viable, there is no due date associated with it). "I was not ready for that. I don't think you're ever ready for these ritual moments in Judaism. They don't have flexibility. It meant that I had to do some work to get myself there," she remembered. In her role as clergy, Sarah was in charge of leading her community through these ritual services and memorial prayers even in the midst of coping with her own grief. When I commented on how hard that must have been, she responded, "It's a gift to be able to create space and support people in their healing."

When the first anniversary of Sarah's abortion came, she expected the day to bring back intense feelings of grief, but to her surprise, it didn't. "I already felt like I had made my abortion a part of myself. I didn't feel the trauma anymore. It amazed me that a year after the abortion, I already felt I had done the healing work I needed to start speaking and advocating," she shared. Prior to her ectopic pregnancy, Sarah was engaged in advocacy work for reproductive freedom, in part because of experiences that took place in her extended family, but now she had her own story to tell of why access to abortion is essential health care.

Sarah told me, "I never thought I was pregnant. I just felt like I had lost a pregnancy." She never got to decide if she would continue the pregnancy or not. When I asked her if she considered what happened to her an abortion, she was adamant that it was. Her major cause of concern now is the real possibility that she may need to access the same kind of abortion care again in the future. The biggest risk factor for having an ectopic pregnancy is already having had one.

You might be wondering why Sarah would have this fear of not getting the care she needs. Her life and health were clearly at risk. Wouldn't any physician perform the necessary abortion procedure she would need to preserve her life? Unfortunately, that is not the case everywhere. In some rural areas, the only available hospital is associated with the Catholic Church. All of these facilities are subject to the Ethical and Religious Directives for Catholic Health Care Services, under which an ectopic pregnancy cannot be treated through "direct abortion." This means that treatments like the ones Sarah received—the injection and the surgery—would be unavailable to patients there. Religiously affiliated hospitals and providers are permitted legally to deny medical care under religious refusal clauses. Proponents of these exemptions argue that they are protected under the right to religious liberty in the Constitution. Legal arguments based on "religious freedom" have been successful in upholding these refusals. In multiple instances in recent years, the Supreme Court has sided in favor of restrictions to reproductive care and denial of services to LGBTQ+ individuals under this premise. But for people like Sarah, access to abortion is essential to *their* religious freedom. Under Jewish law, abortion is not just permissible but actually mandated in some instances. In Sarah's case, even under the narrowest interpretation of Jewish law, her religion demanded that she end the pregnancy to preserve her own life.

Religiously affiliated medical facilities are not the only barrier to necessary reproductive health care, including abortion. There are also ill-informed politicians like Ohio Republican state lawmaker Rep. John Becker, who spread dangerous misinformation about reproductive health and pregnancy. In December 2009, Becker consulted a lobbyist for the Right to Life Action Coalition of Ohio to craft a bill that would prevent insurance companies from covering abortion procedures, except for ectopic pregnancies that could be "reimplanted" into the uterus. Astoundingly, Rep. Becker admitted he never did any research to confirm if this was a medically sound procedure. If he had, he would have found nothing to back his claim because it is absolutely *not* medically sound. He said, "I heard about [the procedure] over the years. I never questioned it or gave it a lot of thought."[4] These dangerous political stunts mechanized by antiabortion politicians like Rep. Becker are exactly why Sarah knows she cannot move to a state like Ohio. Sarah pointed out not only that he spread dangerous misinformation but also that he demonstrated a complete lack of compassion and sensitivity to the people who, like her, have experienced ectopic pregnancies and would have done anything to make such a procedure possible.

Sarah told me that she wants to be a parent. She would have been overjoyed if that pregnancy had been viable. Despite her surgery, she is still hopeful that one day she will have a healthy pregnancy, but she is also mindful of the reality that she might need another abortion in the future to save her life again. She told me, "I wouldn't wait until my life was in danger to protect my health. I am putting myself first. I'm only going to live in a place where I can get the care that I need, which restricts the kinds of communities I am able to serve. But communities in other places need advocates and clergy who are compassionate too."

Sarah is right. Every community needs people of faith advocating for abortion care as essential health care and lifting up the fact that unhindered access to comprehensive reproductive health care both upholds human rights and protects our constitutional right to religious freedom. As I reflected on my conversation with Sarah, I thought about another woman I spoke with who lives in Mississippi, a state notoriously hostile toward reproductive freedom. Her story brings us face-to-face with the struggle of accessing abortion care in a place where reproductive rights are on the chopping block every legislative session.

Alexandra, Mississippi

Names have been changed to protect the family's privacy.

> "I don't have any regrets about my abortion. I never feel like a member of our family is missing. It would have been nice to have a third child, but I don't have any guilt or lingering sadness that we didn't have the one that came to us that third time."

In 2011, the citizens of Mississippi prepared to vote on a state constitutional amendment touted by antiabortion activists that defined "personhood" as beginning at the moment of fertilization when sperm and egg connect. If adopted, the amendment would have outlawed abortion outright, but it also had the potential to impact much more than that. Access to certain forms of contraception and infertility treatments like in vitro fertilization would have been threatened too. "It was so extreme and ridiculous," Alexandra told me. She hadn't been political in the past, but this proposed constitutional amendment pushed her to take action. She knew she had to do her part to stop it from becoming state law. She got connected with reproductive freedom activists on the ground and joined an online community of parents working against the amendment, which ultimately failed. What Alexandra didn't realize was that her advocacy work at the time would prepare her for an expected reproductive decision she would need to make just a few years later.

In 2007, four years before the Mississippi personhood amendment was proposed, Alexandra was in the middle of a long, grueling labor with her first child. She described the experience to me as a dark night of the soul, a time of not only physical exhaustion but also spiritual crisis. "I felt like I was in hell, and I was never going to get out of it," she told me. "I was not spiritually equipped to descend into that underworld." At 3:00 a.m., Alexandra mustered up her remaining strength to give one last push that brought her baby boy Henry into the world. Exhausted and depleted from labor, she fell into a much-needed deep sleep as the nursing staff tended to her newborn son. Four hours later, they woke her up abruptly. Something was wrong with Henry, they told her. There was possibly a complication with his heart, and he would need to be airlifted to the closest hospital with a NICU immediately. Alexandra and her husband, Bryan, would have to follow in an ambulance. The drive was over a hundred miles.

Doctors in the NICU diagnosed Henry with neonatal alloimmune thrombocytopenia (NAIT), a rare blood-related disorder that causes a fetus or newborn to have a low platelet count. It is a condition only detected after birth, and it's potentially fatal, as she would later learn. While a medical team monitored her baby carefully in the NICU, Alexandra recovered from the birth a few floors away in the maternity ward. Thankfully, Henry responded well to treatment, and four days after his birth, he was released from the hospital. After a frightening and traumatic beginning to their parenting journey, Alexandra and Bryan were grateful that their baby boy was well enough to bring him home.

Alexandra shared just how much she and Bryan fell in love with their baby and how taking care of him together deepened their love for each other. They knew they wanted to grow their family in the future, but they worried about the potential risks. When would they be ready emotionally for what might happen with another pregnancy and birth? What health complications might arise the second time around, and how would they handle them? When she brought her concerns to her doctors, she told me that they did not discourage her from a future pregnancy. They reassured her that they would be prepared to handle any potential health complications and intervene early if necessary. She would likely need to deliver by cesarean section, they told her, but there was no reason for Alexandra to believe that a healthy pregnancy and delivery was out of reach.

Six years after Henry's birth, Alexandra and Bryan were expecting their second child. They'd moved to a new town, and Alexandra found a new ob/gyn. She shared with me that when she was look-ing for a new provider, she chose her doctor in part because he had been a vocal opponent to the proposed "personhood" amendment. After learning of Henry's NAIT, her physician said that he wanted to take every necessary precaution to avoid these same complications. About midway through her pregnancy, Alexandra took a blood test that confirmed her fetus was at risk of the same blood disorder that Henry had at birth.

Her doctor was taking no chances and prescribed her a weekly regi-men of intravenous immunoglobulin, which is made up of antibodies collected from thousands of blood donors. Alexandra told me that it's referred to as "liquid gold" because of its high cost; a single treatment can run a patient thousands of dollars. Since it also requires several hours to be administered, many patients have to spend the night at the hospital, an additional cost. Alexandra was fortunate to have health insurance and financial resources to receive this treatment weekly, but even so, it was a hardship for her family. For months she had to spend one night every week at the hospital, which was hard on her family and especially disruptive to her young son. "I didn't realize I was signing up for this," she said. "We were on a roller coaster, and we just had to keep riding it."

The plan had been for Alexandra to make it to thirty-eight weeks before having a scheduled C-section, but in her third trimester, she developed preeclampsia, a potentially dangerous and even fatal con-dition that can cause significant damage to the liver and kidneys of a pregnant person. She shared that as part of her treatment for the NAIT her fetus might have, she had to take steroids, which likely contributed to her preeclampsia. She was also grieving the death of her best friend, who had passed away suddenly. At thirty-six weeks, Alexandra delivered her second son, Charlie, by C-section, thankfully without additional complications. The hospital staff were vigilant in checking the newborn for any sign of NAIT, but the intense treatments during Alexandra's pregnancy worked as expected. Charlie was perfectly healthy.

Caring for a new baby and raising a child with special needs (Henry had been diagnosed with autism spectrum disorder) were rewarding but exhausting. Alexandra said that it was challenging to make time for anything else, including doctor's appointments for herself. Any parent would be overwhelmed with caring for two young children, but Alexandra has the additional challenge of living with attention deficit hyperactivity disorder (ADHD), which increases feelings of worry and overwhelm and makes accomplishing tasks difficult. While she knew that she needed to be on some kind of contraceptive, she did not have the mental bandwidth to take care of it. Bryan and Alexandra used condoms, a contraceptive method that is typically about 85 percent effective.[5] In 2016, three years after Charlie's birth, Alexandra discovered she was pregnant for a third time.

In most areas of her life, Alexandra is indecisive. "Unless I have a strong preference, I don't have a preference," she explained. But when the pregnancy test was positive, she had an immediate, absolute knowledge that she could not continue this pregnancy. She had just weaned Charlie, and she could not imagine going through the ordeal all over again, spending all of those nights at the hospital receiving treatments and possibly ending up with preeclampsia a second time.

Her boys needed her. Her husband needed her. She needed to take care of herself, and she knew she needed an abortion. "I couldn't believe those words were coming into my mind," she recalled. Even though she had advocated for the pro-choice cause, she never imagined being in a position of needing an abortion herself. But she was firm in her decision. She told her husband that she was pregnant and that she couldn't have this baby.

Alexandra turned to the network of advocates she had gotten to know in 2011 when she advocated against the personhood amendment. Offers of support poured in. "I knew if I had any problems, I had people I could ask for help," she told me. She had joined a mothers' group on Facebook and read a post from a Unitarian Universalist minister about abortion and miscarriage. The minister shared an insight that Alexandra found helpful: "You're allowed to tell this spirit or soul, 'I'm sorry. You can't come right now. This is not the right time.'" That gave her an even greater sense of peace about her decision to end the pregnancy.

On the day of the first appointment (Mississippi requires two: one for in-person abortion counseling and then another, at least twenty-four hours later, for the procedure), Bryan stayed home with their two boys while a friend accompanied Alexandra to what is now the state's only abortion clinic, Jackson Women's Health Organization. Known to many as the "Pink House" for its bright pink exterior, the clinic is a constant target for antiabortion protesters. Because Alexandra had been to the building before as an advocate defending their work, she was prepared to face whoever might try to stand in her way of receiving abortion care. "I had a sense of how I had to shield myself energetically so that none of the shame [the protesters] wanted to put in me got in," she said.

Alexandra sat with the other patients that day as they went through a state-mandated class about abortion. When she went in to get her ultrasound, Alexandra was so early in her pregnancy that it was undetectable, and she had to return a full week later. Though delaying her second appointment was unexpected and, in her case, a minor inconvenience, Alexandra credits the clinic for their caution: "They weren't going to give me medication I didn't need. They're not just here to make money." After a somewhat difficult week of waiting, Alexandra returned to the clinic—this time on her own—and after detecting her pregnancy through the ultrasound, she got the prescription she needed for her medication abortion, which she needed to fill at a local pharmacy. She briefly wondered if she ought to travel to a nearby town where no one would recognize her. The prescription cost $400, an expense their family could cover, which she recognizes as a rare privilege. She went home, read the instructions several times, and took the medication.

The process of the abortion itself was not difficult for Alexandra physically or emotionally. She'd already been through childbirth twice. She said, "Having years and years to develop my sense of my own bodily autonomy is what informed me to make that decision to end the pregnancy that much more easily." But what did prove difficult was the realization that she could not share what she had gone through freely with her loved ones. Her parents, who are conservative Christians, still do not know about the abortion to this day because Alexandra knows they would not be able to handle it. She said, "I'm an open person, and it takes a lot of work for me not to be. I'm not used to having to shield things." Having to hold this secret carries its own kind of pain and grief.

It's not only her parents that Alexandra is worried about. She wonders what her obstetrician would think if he knew about her abortion. Even though her doctor spoke out against the personhood amendment, she is still not sure how he would react to finding out she'd had an abortion herself. "When you're in a place like Mississippi, when you're not in a safe environment, you never really know how someone is going to respond," she shared. Sometimes she wonders what would have happened if she had complications with her medication abortion. What kind of care would she have gotten at the local hospital when she disclosed her abortion? Afterward, when Bryan scheduled an appointment to have a vasectomy, his doctor actually tried to talk him out of going through with it. He thought to himself, *This guy doesn't know what we've just been through.*

Having an abortion only solidified Alexandra's commitment to the work of justice: "I said to Spirit, I am ready to do this work. What can I do? Use me as you see fit." Today she continues to advocate for reproductive freedom and human rights in Mississippi. Once at a march organized by Black Lives Matter, some white antiabortion protesters were being disruptive during a moment of silence meant to honor the Black victims of police violence. People in the crowd were becoming visibly upset in response to their shouting. Then Alexandra noticed that the cord connected to their speaker was within arm's reach. Wordlessly, she pulled the plug. She said, "It was one of those moments when you know God or Spirit puts you there to use you."

Because of their access to abortion care when they needed it, both Sarah and Alexandra have been able to grow and move forward, incorporating their abortion experiences into the ways that they move throughout the world. Sarah continues to serve as a congregational leader, and she is hoping to share her abortion experience through poetry and song that she will write one day. Alexandra has embraced her role as an advocate in her community and continues to explore the ways that she can support movements for justice. For each of them, the decision to have an abortion was an act of self-compassion and an affirmation that *their* lives were sacred and worth saving in every sense of the word. This is what abundant life looks like.

We ought not expect anyone to justify or apologize for the preservation of their well-being when we know that a life of abundance is the desire and intention of the most Holy for each of us. Access to abortion is essential for our collective flourishing. Even when these decisions are painful and hard, they are ultimately life-giving.

4

FOR SELF-PRESERVATION

Content Warning: This chapter discusses and describes suicidal ideation.

> You have put me in the depths of the Pit, in the regions dark
> and deep.
>
> —Psalm 88: 6

Psalm 88 is a prayer of despair and desperation. "My soul is full of
troubles," the psalmist writes. "I am like those who have no help,
like those forsaken among the dead" (vv. 3–4). I feel the raw descriptions of hopelessness, of feeling forsaken and cut off from God deep
in my soul. These ancient words transport me back to the moment
more than a decade ago when I first received a diagnosis of clinical
depression. Much like the psalmist who likens their condition to a
deep, dark pit, I remember journaling about feeling like I had fallen
into an inescapable hole: the more I tried to pull myself out of it, the

more deeply I fell. It was more than metaphorical. Physically I felt like something or someone was pushing my body down toward the ground, leaving me too worn out to get out of bed some days. I tried everything I could think of to make myself better. I used up every internal and external resource, anything that I had turned to in the past when I was feeling down or discouraged: exercising regularly, getting enough sleep, journaling what I was feeling, and talking to supportive friends and family. Nothing I tried helped lift me out of that deep place. I knew I needed professional help.

Just like experiences of abortion, having a mental health disorder like depression is common; one in five adults in the United States experiences some form of mental health illness every year.[1] More than half of all adults will receive a mental health diagnosis in their lifetime.[2] Unfortunately, many people who need mental health care never access it. First, there is the barrier of cost. Those most in need of services are less likely to have health insurance.[3] A single one-hour therapy session can cost anywhere from $65 to $250 and up. Paying out of pocket isn't feasible if you're unemployed, or underpaid, or living paycheck to paycheck. At the time of my diagnosis, I was working full time as an independent contractor and was ineligible for benefits, including health insurance coverage. I identified a therapist who offered fees on a sliding scale based on income, which I could afford out of pocket. Otherwise, I'm not sure how I would have gotten the care I needed.

Economic injustice is a significant barrier, but it's not the only obstacle. Similar to the stigma of abortion, there is a widespread stigma associated with having a mental health issue. This discourages people from seeking help or even recognizing that they have a disorder at all. Mistrust in the mental health care system also plays a role. The roots of the field are steeped in anti-Black ideology, and that deeply embedded racism continues to shape the field today. Black individuals with mental health disorders are more likely to be misdiagnosed, undiagnosed, underdiagnosed, or incarcerated for their condition.[4] The fields of psychology, social work, and psychiatry are overwhelmingly white. Less than 5 percent of all professionals in these roles are women of color.[5]

These multiple and intersecting obstacles to mental health care prevent far too many people from getting the services they need. The same types of barriers exist for most people who seek abortion care. Our lived experiences with mental illness and disorders, much like our experiences of abortion, often remain shameful secrets. The hiddenness of these lived realities often stands in the way of the healing process. When I asked interviewees about what has helped them find healing after their abortions, the most common response was therapy. The stories I share in this chapter will reveal how access to abortion and access to mental health care are intertwined.

Before turning to these stories, though, we need to be mindful of one of the central (and false) premises of the antiabortion movement: that terminating a pregnancy causes long-term emotional trauma and distress. This is a flat-out lie. Let me reiterate once again that no scientific study has ever confirmed that abortion causes any long-term mental health issues—not in the immediate aftermath of an abortion or in the years after one.

But the pro-life insistence on this correlation between abortion and mental health prompted me to ask a more pressing question: Are there mental health risks in *not* having an abortion when one is needed?

Given my own experience of depression and anxiety during and after pregnancy, as well as what I heard during the interviews for this book, I wanted to know if there were mental health risks for those who want to end a pregnancy but who, for whatever reason, are unable to obtain abortion care. I turned to one of the most comprehensive studies on the short-term and long-term impacts of abortion care, the Turnaway Study, to shed some light on this question. Directed by Dr. Diana Greene Foster and managed by a team of scientists across multiple disciplines, the Turnaway Study followed one thousand women, who either had received abortion care or were denied it, over a period of ten years. Dr. Foster, a professor of reproductive sciences at the University of California and director of research at Advancing New Standards in Reproductive Health (ANSIRH), tests the assertion that abortion hurts those who have them. The data from the study soundly refute the claim that abortion leads to increased rates of mental health disorders. What the study does show, however, is that being *denied* an abortion leads to increased rates of anxiety and stress and lowered rates of life satisfaction and self-worth. Dr. Foster concludes, "To the extent that abortion causes mental health harm, the harm comes from the denial of services, not the provision."[6]

In reading the Turnaway Study, another question emerged for me. Postpartum depression affects about one in eight individuals post-birth,[7] but what about depression *during* pregnancy? Was the state of pregnancy itself a risk factor for new or recurrent mental health issues? Studies on antenatal, or before birth, depression and anxiety have estimated that anywhere between 7 percent and 20 percent of pregnant people experience these conditions at some point. While rates of mental health issues among those who are pregnant are similar to those who are not, pregnant people who have a history of abuse, lack a supportive partner and/or social support, experience other stressful life events, or are having an unintended pregnancy are at an increased risk for mental health disorders while pregnant—and those who have experienced mental illness previously are especially vulnerable to recurrences and/or intensification of these conditions during pregnancy.[8] One storyteller, who has bipolar disorder and whose story I will share in another chapter, brought this home for me: "Before I even knew I was pregnant, I was hit with a wave of depression where I couldn't get out of bed for three days. Pregnancy was not livable for me. When you have bipolar disorder, pregnancy hormones work against your medication. If I had continued the pregnancy, I would have had to go off of my mood stabilizers. If someone had taken those from me, I would've died. I would not have lived to give birth." For Heidi and Jeana, whose stories are included in this chapter, the experience of having an abortion was not the cause of their mental health issues. In Heidi's case, it was the pregnancy as well as the circumstances surrounding it that triggered preexisting conditions and exacerbated her struggles. For Jeana, having a therapist helped her work through the layers of feelings she had about her life at the time, including her abortion experience. Access to both mental health care and abortion care was essential to their overall well-being—in particular, their mental and spiritual wellness. While their experiences vary in degree of severity, they both speak to the necessity of having access to a full range of health care services in order to heal from loss and trauma and experience wholeness in their lives.

Heidi Howes, Columbus, Ohio

"It can be the right decision even when it hurts."

What started for Heidi as a wanted and planned pregnancy suddenly became a living nightmare. It was the end of 2013, and she was only a few weeks pregnant when she experienced a rapid, frightening decline in her physical and mental health. She described her state of mind at the time like this: "Every day I woke up and the first thought in my head was about how I was going to kill myself that day." I had heard others talk about severe depression during pregnancy, but Heidi was the first to describe the gravity of her illness in such frank terms. From our conversation, I could tell how much she loves being a mother to her two children and how much she wanted a third child. She still does today. But she knew that she would not survive nine months of constant suicidal thoughts. "I had to save myself," she said.

She shared about her previous pregnancies and the trauma surrounding them. When Heidi was twenty-seven, she was in a committed relationship with a man whom she loved and planned to marry when she discovered that she was pregnant. They were both happy and excited about starting a family together. Heidi's partner suffered from severe bipolar disorder, and while he had been forthcoming about his condition, Heidi had yet to witness the extent of his mental illness. During her first trimester, he had a violent psychotic episode after abruptly stopping his mood-stabilizing medication. Shocked and traumatized by what she had witnessed, Heidi fled to a women's shelter.

In the aftermath of that trauma, she questioned if continuing her pregnancy was the right thing to do. Could she ever recover from what happened and stay in a romantic relationship with this person? What would it mean to parent a child while caring for someone with a severe and at times volatile mental illness? As she considered what to do, she spoke with her circle of trusted friends, many of whom told her about abortions they had in the past. One of them said to her, "Heidi, you could end this pregnancy, but I could also see you being an amazing parent regardless of what happens to your relationship." Heidi did schedule an appointment to have an abortion, but in the end, she never went in for the procedure. She decided to continue her pregnancy, even if that meant she would be parenting alone.

Later that year, Heidi gave birth to a healthy baby boy and later married her partner. From the outside, they looked like a happy family, but Heidi was the one holding their life together. She was a full-time caretaker of both her child and her mentally ill husband, all while she single-handedly struggled to earn enough money to support them.

Despite her enormous caretaking load and lack of support at home, Heidi sought all of the resources that she could to care for her own mental health. Throughout her adult life, she had suffered from bouts of depression. Over the years, she worked closely with therapists, sticking with treatment even when she struggled to see the benefit, and took antidepressants. Because of these experiences, she told me, "I thought I had mastered my depression. I thought I knew what to look out for. I thought I knew the warning signs." But after the life-threatening labor and delivery of their second child, which lasted more than three days and ended in an emergency C-section, Heidi was beyond depleted. Soon after the birth of her daughter, she rapidly fell into a postpartum depression so severe that she spent over a month in the hospital receiving psychiatric treatment.

In 2010, Heidi ended the marriage with her children's father. She knew that this would impact her kids' relationship with him, but she wanted and deserved more: a real partnership rooted in mutuality. A year after her separation, Heidi found herself in another toxic relationship, this time with an abusive, controlling man. "I felt like I was under some kind of spell," Heidi said. "I knew that the relationship was toxic and I wasn't supposed to be in it, but at the same time I was also *in* the relationship." She couldn't see a way out.

Two years into their relationship, Heidi and this new partner decided that they wanted to have a child together. After experiencing a miscarriage, Heidi conceived a second time. Quickly she realized that there was something different about this pregnancy—and not in a good way. Within a few weeks, she was feeling so fatigued and depressed that she could not get out of bed. "I couldn't get my bearings," she said. "I was in a fog." Her partner didn't show her any sympathy; he berated her for being tired all of the time and not going to work.

Heidi knew that she needed professional help, but she couldn't afford it. Her Medicaid insurance had lapsed, and there was no money to pay for therapy. She was pregnant, depressed, and in a toxic relationship—all while she continued to take care of her two children.

"I was caring for others when I needed to be cared for," she told me. Even though she wanted another baby, she had to make a decision for her own life and for the lives of the children she already had. When he found out about her decision to end the pregnancy, Heidi's partner became enraged. He screamed at her, "You're killing our baby! You're killing *my* baby!" The emotional abuse continued to escalate, but in spite of the threats and manipulation, Heidi was resolved in her decision to have an abortion. What she needed was help paying for it.

One of the biggest barriers to abortion care is the cost, especially for low-income people. Advocates for reproductive justice have been working for years to bring an end to the Hyde Amendment, enacted by Congress every year since 1976, which prohibits the use of federal funds for abortion services except in the cases of rape, incest, and life endangerment. This means that anyone who is insured through Medicaid or any other federally funded health program has no coverage for abortion, which directly impacts young people, poor people, communities of color, and other marginalized groups. In Heidi's case, she had the support of her mother, who was willing and able to help come up with the $800 she needed. So many others have nowhere to turn.

Heidi's appointment at the health center was positive and relatively uneventful, but she told me that she was surprised by how clinical it was. "There was no one there whose role was to help me heal," she said. Sitting in the waiting room, Heidi connected with some of the other patients who were there to have abortions, most of whom were parents too. (In fact, the majority of people who get abortions are already parents.[9]) As she prepared to go back for her procedure, a song popped into her head: "I Will," a Beatles song covered by Allison Krauss. I wasn't familiar with it, so Heidi sang a few lines for me. It was beautiful in that kind of haunting yet calming way with lyrics about how love remains forever, across time and space. She told me that she hadn't thought of the song in years and remembering it at that very moment felt like a sign of comfort that had been sent to soothe her.

A week after her abortion, Heidi went to visit a friend in Maine. She finally had some space to breathe. As the pregnancy hormones left her body, the depression started to lift, and her thoughts became clearer. "I could see that this man was not for me, and I could never have a child with him," she said. She recalled a couple's counseling session they once had when their therapist, a military veteran who worked with incarcerated people, said to her privately, "You need to run as fast as you can from this man. He is one of the most antisocial people I have ever seen, and he's not going to change." Now that the pregnancy was over, she could see the truth for what it was: he would have used their child to control and manipulate her.

Reproductive coercion is a common way that abusers attempt to control their partners, as Heidi's had done when she shared her plan to end the pregnancy. Abortion access is critical to addressing and ending gender-based violence because those who are *denied* abortion care are more likely to stay in a toxic relationship.[10] After her abortion, Heidi left her abuser, and her psychological health stabilized. She has not had a depressive episode since.

Even though Heidi's abortion was more than five years ago, she shared with me that it still feels raw when she thinks about it. Now Heidi is in a loving relationship and feels ready to welcome a third child into her life. There are moments when she wonders what would have happened if she had just pushed through that pregnancy: "What if I had sacrificed more?" But when those thoughts come up, she recognizes that those are opportunities to deepen her own healing and self-compassion.

We ended our conversation with a rich discussion about the divine and our spiritual practices. She shared this amazing experience she had not long after her abortion when during a time of ritual, she had a vision of what she described as the "divine mother." During the encounter, this presence shared with Heidi that her abortion was a "medicine you have to carry" in order to help others heal. Since that time, Heidi has become an energy healer and a shamanic practitioner. She worked with spiritual mentors and trained in Reiki, a form of therapy to move energy around the body and promote healing and pain relief. Today she offers her spiritual services to individuals and to her community through the nonprofit she cofounded called Motherful, which works to connect with and provide resources to single mothers in the Columbus area.

Heidi knows that her sacred purpose in this life is to help others heal, but before she could help anyone else, she needed to do her own work first. She commented, "Many of us come to healing work and helping others because we don't have a sense of a separate self. It's true that in helping others heal, we are healed. But I first had to do my own healing for things to begin to click. I came into healing work because I needed to heal myself."

Who among us is not in need of some kind of healing? We all go through painful experiences in our lives that leave wounds and need our loving attention. Looking at these places takes courage, and releasing old thought patterns, behaviors, and relationships takes an enormous amount of courage. We are conditioned to believe that choosing ourselves is an act of selfishness when in fact it is often an act of faith—and a pathway to helping others find their healing.

Jeana Nam, Houston, Texas

> "I feel very grateful for the abortion that I had. It was life-defining for me in a lot of ways. The fact that I was making a decision about my life, my body, and my future on my own, not needing permission from anyone else, was a powerful experience for me. It also set me on this life path that I would never have pursued if it weren't for my own lived experience."

One of the first things I noticed when Jeana and I connected over Zoom was a tattoo on the inside of her forearm. I was particularly interested because I'd just gotten my first ink, an American robin, earlier that month. After catching a glance of hers a few times, I could make out that it was some kind of bird. I'd intended to ask her about its significance, but then I got so swept up in our conversation that I forgot to bring it up. The following day, just as I sat down to write Jeana a quick thank-you email, one from her popped into my inbox:

> Almost immediately after we ended our call, I realized I had more to say! I have a tattoo in the shape of the Repeal Hyde[11] bird with the words "you are sacred" written inside of it. I had gone through phases of deconstructing my faith prior to my abortion, and afterward I started to seek a theology to fill the space that this deconstruction had left. I felt drawn toward theological frameworks that emphasized embodiment and life here on earth, rather than the disembodied soul and heaven. My experiences in the reproductive justice movement, as well as my personal abortion

experience, have led me to see the body (particularly nonwhite, non-cis male bodies) as sacred and worth protecting.

Jeana grew up in College Station, Texas, a predominantly white and conservative evangelical community where the antiabortion campaign 40 Days for Life got its start. Jeana described the church of her childhood not as a stereotypical "fire and brimstone, Bible-thumping" kind of congregation that many people associate with evangelicalism but rather as one where the focus was on grace ("Grace was even in the name of the church," Jeana shared). The trouble was that the messages about vulnerability, community, and grace that were preached from the pulpit didn't line up with the community's actual practices. They used loving language, but they didn't implement it.

At Jeana's church, being antiabortion was implied, not explicit. The congregation supported crisis pregnancy centers, and the strong presence of 40 Days for Life in the town was impossible to ignore. Being pro-life was just a given. Once, Jeana's mother halfheartedly joked about having an abortion if she were to get pregnant again. "I was scandalized," Jeana remembered, chuckling. "I was twelve years old, and I got on my soapbox to say, 'Mom, you can't say things like that. That's terrible.'" I laughed as I remembered my own clueless self-righteousness at that age. By the time Jeana got to high school, her political views had changed, and she started to question and examine what she'd been taught about God and life at church.

What she didn't question was the love and care of her church friends. As we talked more about her abortion, the loss she felt had little to do with the decision itself and much more to do with the fear of losing her community and closest relationships. "The grief I felt was knowing that [my abortion] was going to change significant relationships in my life, *even if I never told them,*" she said. In spite of the fact that her faith community preached about the beauty of vulnerability and the unconditional love of God, she knew that her particular abortion story would not be deemed acceptable in their sight. In order to fit into their theological framework, she said, "You have to have certain feelings about your abortion for your experience to be viewed as legitimate by the community and for your faith to be seen as authentic." Unless she was willing to say that her abortion was wrong and that she regretted it, there wouldn't be a place for her. Much of the healing she has done in the aftermath of her abortion has to do with reconciling her relationship with the church, a journey that she is still on now.

Jeana had taken a break from college in order to deal with some mental health issues she was experiencing. She was working with a therapist, seeking answers to the questions she had about her future. Two years ago, she had entered college with the plan to become a doctor, but once it became clear that was not the right path for her, she was feeling lost. One day, when her mom was visiting, Jeana mentioned some nausea she'd felt. Her mom offhandedly asked, "Are you pregnant? You should get a pregnancy test." As it turns out, Jeana was pregnant. She scheduled her abortion right after Thanksgiving, and while Jeana was home with family, she kept her pregnancy and scheduled termination to herself.

When I asked how she felt during that time, Jeana answered that she mostly blocked it out. She was focused on getting the procedure done. There was a clinic close to campus, a popular location for abortion protesters. "I remember it was really crowded inside the clinic, but I felt really cared for," she recalled. At seven weeks pregnant, she opted for a procedure over a medication abortion, and when it was done, her partner drove her home and brought her an orchid, a gesture of love and support. The following day, Jeana put the abortion behind her and resumed her daily life.

Jeana never felt any regret about her abortion, but she still had to deal with the "scripts" about abortion that she'd picked up at church. She didn't know anyone who'd had an abortion, and she didn't tell anyone about hers. For several months she managed to avoid thinking much about it. Then one day she read a column about someone who had a miscarriage, and it triggered all sorts of emotions and doubts. She went to her therapy appointment in tears, wondering if she had killed her baby. Her therapist helped normalize the abortion experience. Knowing it would be helpful for Jeana, they had a discussion about the science of fetal development. Together they sorted through all of Jeana's feelings and questions that finally had risen to the surface. She told Jeana, "You don't have to hold onto these stories anymore. They don't serve you." As she began to let go of the stories and the scripts of her childhood, all of her lingering doubts and difficult feelings about her abortion dissipated.

When I asked Jeana how she thinks of her abortion now, she told me she sees the experience as sacred. It was a life-defining moment for her, and she described it as "the first major decision I made for myself as an adult." This experience set Jeana on a life path that she never anticipated. She began volunteering with reproductive justice organizations in Texas and started working as a counselor at the same clinic where she'd had her procedure. Later she became a public storyteller with We Testify and shared that while some of her church friends haven't accepted her story, others have. She has found another community through her reproductive justice work too. When we talked, she was about to start graduate school in mental health counseling. Jeana has always felt a calling to help others; her abortion helped her discern what path that would take.

Jeana shared a piece she wrote entitled "I Hope the Christian Church Makes Room for Abortion Stories like Mine":

> I am a Christian, and I had an abortion. Experiences like mine were never discussed in the evangelical community I grew up in, which was riddled with stigmatizing rhetoric and shame about abortion that unfortunately persists today.
>
> Before and after my abortion, I experienced painful emotional distress from the fear of judgment and isolation I felt, having gone through an experience few of my friends would understand or support. There was no doubt in my mind that I had made the right decision for myself, and I felt immense relief in the days after my abortion, but it was still difficult for me to distinguish that personal grief from the anti-abortion rhetoric I had internalized in my childhood.
>
> Not only is my faith consistent with my beliefs about abortion and true justice, it also drives my activism. I want to ensure that no one is shamed or punished for making decisions based on their own conscience and knowing what's best for them. When I served as a patient counselor at Houston Women's Clinic, an independent abortion provider, I spoke with countless people who identified as anti-abortion because of their religious beliefs

but who ultimately believed that God would understand their own decision to end their pregnancy. I've chosen to share my story this Lenten season because I want people who have had abortions—whatever their faith or spiritual beliefs—to know that they are not alone, and there is no right or wrong way to feel about your abortion.

My faith is still deeply important to me; it just looks different than it did in my childhood. I wouldn't trade my church upbringing for the world. I know that there are other stories out there like mine. I have hope that the church will make room for them someday.[12]

We have seen how a pregnancy, even one that is wanted, can trigger a psychological emergency. Having the ability to make critical decisions about our bodies, families, and futures is essential to our mental well-being and our overall flourishing as individuals, families, and communities. And sometimes ending a pregnancy truly is a matter of life or death.

5

FOR THE DIGNITY OF YOUNG PEOPLE

How does God's love abide in anyone who has the world's goods
and sees a brother or sister in need and yet refuses help? Little
children, let us love, not in word or speech, but in truth and action.

—1 John 3:17–18

As I detail in my first book, *Women Rise Up*, my relationship with
Mary, the mother of Jesus, is complex. This has less to do with the
biblical account of her life and more to do with the ways that she
has been idealized and her story sanitized. We tend to dismiss her
young age and forget the fact that being unmarried and pregnant
was shameful, risky, and even dangerous. We overlook the state of
her actual pregnancy and skip past the agony of her labor, neglecting how she first gave of *her* body and *her* blood to conceive, gestate,
and birth Jesus safely and lovingly into the world. We forget that at
the very beginning, she gave her consent to become a parent of the

divine: "Here am I, the servant of the Lord; let it be with me according to your word" (Luke 1:38). The biblical text does not tell us that God first consulted Mary's parents or her betrothed Joseph about the possibility of this pregnancy. This was her decision to make about her body and her future.

If we consider this central Christian story through the lens of a young person who gives consent, what might it offer us as we consider the reproductive freedom of pregnant youth today? How might our laws and policies change if we prioritized the autonomy and decision-making of young people, especially pregnant young people?

For the majority of young people under eighteen who need abortions, getting access is tough. Though laws differ state by state, most places require some type of parental involvement for a minor to obtain abortion care, whether through parental consent, parental notification, or both prior to their procedure. Of the twenty-one states that currently require parental consent, eight of them require notarized documentation, and three of them require the consent of both parents.[1] Stop to think about what this process entails and demands of teenagers. Consider the possible complications and even dangers of a child having to share with their parents about their sexuality, pregnancy, and decision to have an abortion.

If a young person living in one of these states cannot obtain consent from their parent(s) or guardian, the only way they can access an abortion is to obtain a judicial bypass, which requires the cumbersome task of navigating the court system and pleading their case before a judge. Again, just imagine what is being required of these young people in order to access abortion care, standing in a courtroom and hoping to be shown compassion and understanding. Judges can deny a bypass for any reason. In the state of Texas in 2018, where two of the stories in this chapter take place, judges ruled to deny minors a judicial bypass in about 13 percent of all cases.[2]

Denying young people confidential, dignified, and comprehensive reproductive health care is reproductive oppression. Coercion of any kind, even if supposedly done in the best interest of a young person, is a violation of their human rights and the divine right that we each have to make moral decisions about our lives. Many doctors agree that confidential abortion care for young people ought to be a protected right. The American Academy of Pediatrics has taken an official stance against parental notification laws because interfering with teens' reproductive health endangers their overall health and well-being. Their organizational position states, "There is no evidence that mandatory parental involvement results in the benefits to the family intended by the legislation. No studies show that forced disclosure results in improved parent-child relationships, improved communication, or improved satisfaction with the decision about the pregnancy outcome."[3] It goes on to say that while many minors voluntarily consult their parents and/or other trusted adults in making their decision to end a pregnancy, laws that force parental involvement can have a negative impact on family dynamics. Adolescents who come from dysfunctional families fear that telling their parents about their pregnancy would escalate familial conflict and violence. They're right to be concerned. Studies have shown violence in abusive families increases when any member is pregnant.[4]

Legal restrictions harm young people and diminish their moral agency. What they need and deserve is the support of informed, trusted adults who can help guide them and provide resources as they make decisions about their bodies and their futures, whether that's accessing abortion, choosing adoption, or deciding to parent. When we read the biblical account of Mary's pregnancy, we see that she is not left alone to figure things out. The angel points her directly to her older cousin Elizabeth, who is also pregnant at the time and could offer support, care, and a safe place to stay. When Mary arrives, she doesn't pass judgment or ask nosy questions; she greets her cousin with love.

Showing compassion to young people means that we shift our focus away from controlling their reproductive lives and toward understanding how we can be better allies to them. We can work to ensure that they get access to the resources, education, and support they need to make healthy decisions based on accurate information and their own inner knowing. Our role is to teach and model that kind of sacred decision-making from the time they are born, and that starts with providing age-appropriate, fact-based sexuality education.

Comprehensive sexuality education is critical to ensuring that every young person, and people of all ages, can make informed decisions based on their own conscience and values about their sexuality and reproductive lives. One of the best models is the holistic Our Whole Lives (OWL) program, developed by the Unitarian Universalist Association and the United Church of Christ, which offers age-appropriate curricula starting with children as young as kindergarten and going all the way to education for older adults. At every age, the program emphasizes "self-worth, sexual health, responsibility, justice, and inclusivity."[5] OWL is as much about developing self-knowing as it is about science.

Young people also need access to confidential, affordable health services like contraception counseling, testing for sexually transmitted infections (STIs), mental health care, and yes, abortion care. When we equip young people with the tools and support they need, we affirm them as moral agents and set them up to make decisions that best align with their values.

In this chapter, I'll be sharing the stories of Lori, Veronika, and CoWanda, who faced obstacles in making decisions about pregnancies when they were in their teens. While Lori had her abortion many years ago, and Veronika and CoWanda had their abortions within the last few years, each of their experiences points to how often young people's needs are silenced by the systems of power in place that claim to act in their best interests. I hope you are inspired and touched by their honesty as well as moved by their wisdom, resolve, and resilience.

As you take in their stories, remember that God trusted a young girl to make a profoundly sacred reproductive decision. Let us embrace that same spirit of trust and openness with young people today.

Lori Miller, Chico, California

"Nobody grows up gracefully."

More than fifty years have passed since Lori's abortion, yet she still felt twinges of embarrassment bringing to mind what was going on in her young life in 1968. She was just a kid at the time, seventeen years old and fresh out of high school, when she slept with a boy she'd had a crush on. It was her first time having sex, and that very night she had a gut feeling that she was pregnant. Maybe she'd picked up on some of that Catholic guilt from all her years of parochial school. At-home pregnancy tests hadn't been invented yet, but Lori didn't need one. When her period was late, she picked up the phone to confide in a girlfriend that she was pregnant.

Lori comes from an interfaith family. Her father was a Jewish immigrant from Germany who lost most of his family in the Holocaust. Her mother, though not particularly religious, was raised Catholic. Lori grew up going to Catholic school, where she was fully indoctrinated in the church's teachings, including opposition to abortion in all cases. Despite its enormous presence in her life, the Catholic faith never resonated with her on a personal spiritual level, though her connection to God was strong. As a teenager, Lori identified as spiritual but not religious at a time well before the rise of the religiously unaffiliated "nones" in the United States.

After learning of their daughter's pregnancy, Lori's parents called the boy's parents over to their house to discuss it, but the boy himself was nowhere to be found. The whole scene was dramatic, Lori told me. The boy's mother cried and made a snide remark about Catholic school girls always going after her son. But this stereotype hardly applied to Lori. She described herself back then as a lonely teen, immature in many ways, and sexually inexperienced. She said she felt like a "pregnant virgin." Though she didn't say it, I filled in "Like Mary."

The following week was a whirlwind. Lori's father called the local Jewish doctor in town, who confirmed the pregnancy before referring them to another Jewish physician based in Mexico City who could perform an abortion. *Roe v. Wade* was still five years away, and the best option for a safe procedure was to get one outside the United States. Lori was fortunate that her family had the means to travel there. Around Christmastime, she and her parents flew to Mexico and drove to a deserted medical facility. This was where Lori would have her abortion. When they got inside, the only other person there was the doctor himself. He administered a sedative intended to put Lori to sleep, though she remembers waking up in the middle of the procedure and feeling a pulling sensation. Perhaps it was her feet leaving the stirrups on the table, she guessed. Afterward, as her family was getting ready to depart the facility, the doctor said to them solemnly, "None of you will speak of this again."

As we talked, Lori recalled that she was not the only girl in her high school to get pregnant, but as far as she knows, she was the only one who had an abortion. One girl got married and gave birth to a son, she remembered. Another was sent to a home for unwed mothers in San Francisco and placed her daughter for adoption. Lori is still friends with this woman, and she told me that years later, her friend was reunited with her daughter. "It was not a 'happily ever after' situation," Lori said solemnly. In thinking about these different paths each of them took, Lori said, "There is no good answer when you find out that you're pregnant when you're seventeen. You have to make the choice that is best for you, but there is no good answer. Your life is going to go off course for a while." But thanks to her family's resources, Lori did have access to a choice most people did not have at the time: a safe abortion procedure.

I gave Lori a bit of background on the Clergy Consultation Service on Abortion (CCS), and while she is unsure of her doctor's connection with them, I know there was a robust presence of faith organizers in California at the time referring pregnant people to reputable abortion providers and advocating to make abortion legal and accessible. In fact, right around the time that Lori discovered she was pregnant, the Clergy Counseling Service for Problem Pregnancies, based in California, went public with an article in the *Los Angeles Times*. Rev. S. Huw Anwyl, a United Church of Christ minister and organizer of the state chapter, recalled an instant surge in requests for their services: "The day after that story was in the *Times*, I had 293 calls [for abortion referrals]."[6]

The CCS did more than make referrals; they checked up on the providers to make sure their services were safe, sanitary, and compassionate. Members of the consultation traveled to places like Mexico City, one of the popular locations for abortion services outside the United States at the time, where they toured medical facilities, met with doctors, and ensured that the clinics were clean and the procedures were safe.[7] While there is no way of knowing if Lori's doctor was connected with the CCS, she likely directly benefited from the organizing of these compassionate doctors, clergy, and laity. In that way, she was incredibly fortunate.

But in the immediate aftermath of her abortion, Lori did not feel relief. She was struck with grief. "Throughout the whole experience, I was completely passive. I took no responsibility for anything. It was easy for me to feel like I lost my child because I did nothing proactive throughout the whole process," she remembered. Every decision about what happened was made for her by her parents and doctors. She'd had no say in the matter. If given the opportunity to process her pregnancy and what *she* wanted to do, perhaps she would have made a different decision—maybe she would have continued the pregnancy—but she wasn't given the autonomy to make her own choice.

She couldn't talk about her abortion with her parents, and she shared only a little with friends. All alone in her grief, she mourned the loss of her pregnancy and the loss of her agency in the process. She imagined the baby she might have had and gave her a name. Then she started to move forward with her life. She enrolled in community college for two years and went on to complete a degree in social work. Through her studies, she wrote about her complicated feelings about the abortion. In time she got to a place of acceptance about what happened to her at that abandoned medical facility in Mexico City.

As much as she struggled with the abortion, and even though she ought to have had a say in the matter, she ultimately knew that it was the right decision for her at the time. Just a little over a decade later, when Lori was thirty years old, married, and more than ready to start a family, she gave birth to a daughter and named her Kristen Elizabeth, the same name she'd chosen for the daughter she didn't have in her youth. "It was a full-circle healing experience," she told me. "If I had continued that pregnancy in my teens, I wouldn't have the children and grandchildren I have now."

Today Lori works as a therapist in a town not far from where she grew up. I asked her if she ever has clients who want to discuss their own abortion experiences with her and what that's like. She told me that occasionally, a client will disclose a pregnancy that they terminated, but in all of her years of practicing, no client has ever sought her services specifically because they had an abortion. Given the antiabortion rhetoric about emotional trauma after a termination, this was yet another piece of evidence, albeit anecdotal, that abortion is rarely the primary factor in a person's emotional distress. That aside, I did want to know if Lori had any words of wisdom or advice for anyone who might be struggling spiritually with an abortion experience. She offered this insight: "Just because you feel sad doesn't mean it was the wrong decision. I would recommend that you meditate on your feelings and listen to the voice within. To me that voice is the voice of God, and that voice will lead you to peace."

Listen to the voice within. It will lead you to peace.

So many times we discourage people, especially those who are younger in years, not to listen to or trust their inward sense of knowing. But it is the very presence of this voice—whether we call it God, Spirit, our higher self, or something else—that guides us to a place of clarity, truth, and peace about even the most challenging decisions we make in our lives. The difficulties often come when we question our intuition or choose to ignore it altogether.

While Lori's parents orchestrated her reproductive health care, the two young women in the following stories kept their abortions from their families. What I admire so much about them is their resolve to seek out the resources and assistance they needed in order to make the best reproductive decisions for their lives at the time, even when the law tried to stand in their way.

Veronika Granado, San Antonio, Texas

> "I admire myself for being that strong and having to do that completely by myself and not with my family involved."

Veronika was on the brink of an exciting new chapter. She had graduated from high school at the top of her class and was making plans to attend her college orientation when she discovered that she was pregnant. "I was hysterical," she said. "I didn't know what was going to happen." She knew she needed an abortion, but she didn't know how to get one. Veronika lives in Texas, one of thirty-eight states that requires parental notification and consent for minors to get an abortion. She knew getting one of her parents on board was impossible. Her dad lived in a different state, and her relationship with her mom was rocky at best. Veronika didn't want to tell them that she was pregnant in the first place, much less tell them that she needed an abortion.

The only way Veronika could get an abortion was to request a judicial bypass in court. As I shared previously, this undue legal burden on young people can be a nearly insurmountable challenge. The process delays care and creates additional stress by requiring minors—who sometimes are represented by pro bono attorneys but not always—to argue that they are capable of making a reproductive decision on their own. It's up to the appointed judge to determine whether they can access care. As Veronika shared her experience with me, I thought about myself at seventeen years old, preparing to go to college. What would it have felt like to have to plead my case in a courtroom and know that my fate was in the hands of a stranger?

Thankfully, Veronika did not have to go through this process alone. After doing some research, she discovered an organization called Jane's Due Process that specifically works with pregnant minors to provide them with the legal, medical, and financial help they need to access abortion care. She was able to text their staff about her situation confidentially, and they quickly responded with everything that she would need to do, step-by-step. First, she would need to visit a clinic and get an ultrasound. They told her that even if she didn't have the funds, she should go ahead and get the ultrasound done, and they would help her to pay for it. Next, she would need to meet with a lawyer that Jane's Due Process would provide at no cost to figure out a game plan.

Veronika was a little skeptical at first. She had never heard of this organization. Was all of this real? Were they actually going to help her, or was there some kind of catch? She was right to be suspicious. Not every organization that gives off the appearance of helping pregnant people is actually supportive of their decisions. For example, crisis pregnancy centers, or CPCs, are antiabortion organizations that advertise themselves as health clinics. Often, they offer free services like ultrasounds as a means to get pregnant people in the door and then give misinformation to dissuade them from getting an abortion. Unsurprisingly, most CPCs are run by conservative Christian charities.

Following the plan outlined by Jane's Due Process was Veronika's only pathway to care. When she called to schedule the ultrasound, the clinic staff told her there would be no upfront fee—that Jane's Due Process had covered it already. She was relieved and reassured that she could trust this organization to help her. Item by item, Veronika checked off what she needed to do in order to be eligible for the judicial bypass. Staff helped her find most of the money for her procedure through an abortion fund. Abortion funds are organizations that step in where the federal and state governments have opted out, helping people pay for their abortions and sometimes covering other associated costs related to travel, childcare, and missed work. More than eighty funds currently provide this kind of assistance, but in 2019, they were only able to help about one-quarter of all the people who called.[8] The demand far exceeds the resources available.

Veronika's last step before her abortion was getting the judicial bypass. She was referred to a reputable lawyer who would advocate on her behalf before the judge. Two weeks after she first texted the hotline about her situation, a judge granted Veronika the legal exemption she needed to schedule her abortion without parental notification.

Those weeks between discovering she was pregnant and getting her judicial bypass felt like an eternity, especially as she was doing it in secret. With loads of logistics to manage, she had no space to deal with any of her feelings about it all. One of the biggest challenges was paying for her abortion. Jane's Due Process pitched in $200, but she still had to come up with an additional $400. She was a high school student with no job or savings, and she could not turn to her parents for help. Fortunately, she had the support of her partner and his family. They drove her to all the appointments and managed to come up with resources to cover the remaining cost of her procedure, even though it was a financial strain on them. Finally, with the paperwork in hand and the assurance that the abortion would be paid in full, Veronika was able to get her abortion scheduled.

The same day as her medication abortion, just hours after leaving the clinic, Veronika moved from her hometown of McAllen to San Antonio, where she would soon start her new life as a college student. With all she had going on, from moving into an apartment, to finding a job, to enrolling in classes, she didn't have much of a chance to process her abortion experience after the fact either. But she could see that it was having an impact on her life. Her relationship with her partner started to break down. She felt isolated and a little bit ashamed. Some of the religious messages from her childhood started popping into her head. "I thought God was never going to forgive me. But I couldn't tell anyone how I thought I was going to hell," she said. Although Veronika was at peace about her decision to end the pregnancy, the religious beliefs about abortion she had absorbed as a child caused her to doubt herself. More accurately, it dictated her beliefs about what she thought she *should* be feeling about her abortion. Even though she truly believed that she was making the right decision to have an abortion, that self-assurance itself felt wrong to her. She had internalized the idea that the only "right" response to having an abortion was to feel guilty, even though what she felt was not guilt but relief. No matter when we heard it or whether we actually believe it, this kind of toxic theology rooted in judgment and shame can have long-lasting impacts on the ways we view ourselves. When we feel pain, we experience it as divine punishment.

About a year after her abortion, the team at Jane's Due Process connected Veronika with Youth Testify, a project of We Testify that is devoted to young people telling their abortion stories publicly on their own terms. After feeling so isolated in the aftermath of her abortion, Veronika now had the support of a community of peers who understood what she had gone through. She became close friends with another storyteller who talked about how her faith helped her through her abortion. Veronika finally felt ready and equipped to work through her own complicated feelings. In time, she began to heal.

Later Veronika joined the team at Jane's Due Process and helped other young people get the care and support they needed. Though reproductive justice is one of her passions, Veronika is pursuing her professional dreams of becoming a mechanical engineer. When she looks back on her abortion at seventeen, she knows it was the best, most mature decision she has made in her life. In an interview for We Testify, she wrote that her abortion was "a life saver and a blessing," something that ensured she could pursue engineering and create the life for herself that she desired and deserved. She said, "Every day I'm reminded that having an abortion was the best decision I have ever made."[9]

CoWanda Rusk, Houston, Texas

> "My parents didn't know that they loved someone who had an abortion."

Before I started my interview with CoWanda, I could already sense her intimate connection with the divine. From her vibrancy to her convictions, everything about her revealed this inner light of love and truth, evidence of her deep faith and spirituality. Though only twenty-one at the time we spoke, her wisdom was breathtaking.

CoWanda had just moved back into her father's house in west Dallas when we connected. She shared that she'd been a toddler when her parents split up, and her dad got remarried to her stepmom. CoWanda calls her "Mom," since she's been part of her life for as long as she can remember. She went back and forth between her parents' homes, which were radically different households. CoWanda's father had a conversion experience and dedicated himself to serving God and his community through church. At his house, there were high expectations and strict values, a kind of legalism as CoWanda described it. She didn't share many of the details about what that entailed, but it was severe enough that at the age of seventeen, CoWanda broke ties with her father and his wife. They had no contact at all for an entire year.

Living full time with her biological mother was chaotic. They moved three times in a single academic year, and CoWanda grew weary of the constant disruption to her life. She told her mom that she was going to live with a friend, but in truth, she was moving in with an abusive partner. "Terrible things were happening to me physically, sexually, and emotionally in that relationship," she confided. Three weeks before her high school graduation, she discovered that she was pregnant.

She had friends and cousins who'd become parents in their teens. Sometimes, before she was pregnant, she wondered if she wanted to have a baby like they did. When the possibility was a reality, not just an idea, she had a frank conversation with God. "Is this what you want for me, God?" she asked. And in response, she heard, "Is this what *you* really wanted?" She had scholarships to college. She had her whole promising life ahead of her. She didn't want to have a baby right now. She needed an abortion.

Like Veronika, CoWanda is from Texas, and she had to navigate the same cumbersome judicial bypass laws. She shared, "I didn't know enough about abortion, only that I knew I needed one at the time." Once again, Jane's Due Process served as a lifeline, and with their help, she got the care she needed, but the whole legal process felt unjust. In an article she wrote for Rewire, CoWanda asserted, "As a Black woman who has seen the corruption and injustices of our justice system in my own family, I couldn't wrap my head around the idea of going through such a criminalizing experience to access abortion care."[10]

When I asked CoWanda about her abortion experience, she described it as spiritual. As a child, she had watched her mother navigate the medical system, which as a low-income family was never accommodating to them. The abortion clinic was the exact opposite: warm, flexible, and caring. Reflecting on the procedure room, she recalled how the staff were dressed in all white and how she felt "surrounded by angels." She has written about feeling God's presence in the room with her. "Getting an abortion was not the scariest thing I had experienced in life," she shared. Growing up in poverty, being molested as a child, being in an abusive relationship—these were traumas. Her abortion was not.

After the procedure, CoWanda waited for her abuser to pick her up, but the hours went by, and he never showed. Eventually, it was time for the clinic to close. While the staff waited patiently for her to find a ride, for the first time she felt completely alone. Then the realization hit her: if she had continued the pregnancy, she would have been this alone all the time, caring for a baby by herself. "To think that I would feel that sense of isolation and loneliness, with an innocent life that I would have to take care of—I was in no position to be a parent," she stressed.

She needed a way out of this abusive relationship, so after a year of no contact, she decided to reach out to her father. "My dad saw my cry for help and knew what was keeping me there," she remembered. He offered her a job at a Christian camp in Missouri, where she once had been a camper. This was her opportunity to break free. She spent the summer in the beautiful, secluded campus, where she had space to breathe and to just *be*. Beneath the canopy of trees along the shores of the camp's serene lake, she journaled, prayed, and processed everything about her life back in Dallas. As the weeks went by, she felt a growing sense of peace and reconnection with herself, the universe, and God.

Her job at camp was with the kitchen staff. As the team prepared meals, they shared with each other about their lives back home. Everyone was involved in their communities. Whether they were leading youth ministries, working as teachers, or doing volunteer work, all of them lived out their faith in action. CoWanda was inspired and challenged by what she heard. She wanted nothing more than to live into the purpose God had for her life. What was it God was calling her to do? She confided in one of her team members about the abuse and the abortion. She responded to CoWanda's story with love and affirmation: that CoWanda had made the best decision for her life and that sharing her abortion story was important and needed.

Not everything about working at the camp was quite so idyllic. Having been a camper herself, she knew that many of the youth attending the camp came from tough situations. Many of them dealt with poverty, abuse, and food insecurity just like she had. As she listened to the camp counselors talk about God, she found some of their messages harmful and based in shame. She spoke up about her concerns, that they weren't being careful with the ways that they were talking about Christ. They had little understanding of where the kids were coming from. What they needed was love and understanding, not more fear.

No one took her seriously. As a member of the kitchen staff, who were predominantly Black women, she wasn't regarded with the same esteem as the predominantly white staff leaders. Three weeks into the camp season, she was ready to pack up her stuff and head back to Texas. She sent her dad a long email with an idea and a challenge: their family should offer this kind of ministry in west Dallas because they understood the needs of the people. They had the opportunity to share about God in loving, compassionate ways.

Despite her frustrations with some of the power dynamics, CoWanda decided to stay at camp for the rest of the summer. As she was finishing up her time there, she got an email from one of the team members at Jane's Due Process. This happened occasionally—they would reach out with opportunities to volunteer or get more involved. The timing had never felt right. But this message intrigued her. She had been nominated for a storytelling cohort specifically for young people who'd had abortions. She wondered if this was her answer to prayer. Was this what she was supposed to say yes to? One major obstacle stood in her way: the retreat was in Boston. She couldn't afford to get herself there from Missouri. When she learned that everything—her transportation, lodging, and meals—would be taken care of, she took it as a divine sign. She told the team, "I'll be there."

Just days after finishing up her job at the camp, CoWanda attended the first-ever Youth Testify retreat hosted by We Testify. She was a bit apprehensive about participating; she wasn't sure how she would be received by the group. In her conversations with the retreat planning team, they had put a lot of emphasis on the fact that she was a young woman with a strong Christian faith. She worried that she might be stepping into yet another place where she wouldn't be taken seriously. At the camp, when she raised her concerns about the injustices happening there, she was ignored. Would this be more of the same?

When she arrived in Boston and met the other storytellers, she immediately felt an embracing, accepting love from the group. Finally, she was ready and in a place where she could begin to start healing her life. During the retreat, she learned how her personal experience with abortion was connected to a much larger political, social, and historical reality of oppression. She knew this intrinsically—this was what she had tried to name at camp. But the facilitators gave her a framework and a language through which she could start to make sense of her life in a new way. She said that until then, she had known nothing of the reproductive justice movement (which I will talk more about in the next chapter), but it immediately rang true for her. "I learned about why I'd been struggling and about the systemic oppression that exists to hold Black and brown people back," she explained.

I was struck by the truth that what CoWanda had expected to experience at the Christian summer camp she found instead at the Youth Testify retreat. Even though some of the retreat participants were not religious or spiritual, they showed her the love of God. They cared for her, listened to her, and honored her story. She knew that this was the space for which she had prayed: "This was how I was going to achieve my utmost healing and how I was going to get my family on track for healing. This was how I was going to become whole." There at the retreat, among this new community of loving support, she felt moved to share the whole truth about her abortion, and she has been talking about it ever since.

Both camp and the retreat concluded with a call to action: go back to your community and share your truth. With clarity and resolve, she began to tell her faith-filled abortion story with a boldness and a confidence in God's love. At her first public speaking event, one of the founders of Jane's Due Process, an older white man, came to her in tears. He was moved by her story, and he couldn't believe he'd had a hand in saving a young woman's life. And that's exactly what CoWanda's abortion experience did for her: it saved her life.

No longer silenced by shame and stigma, she embraced the unconditional love of God for herself and for all people. She laughed, "The anti-choice people hate me because I thank God for my abortion." She wrote her first public article for *Teen Vogue* and shared it on social media, knowing she would get pushback from Christians in her life. She sighed, "God is so tired of what is holding us in chains." CoWanda knows that her work is to help others break free like she did.

She is determined to keep sharing her story with more and more people. She said, "I have to talk about [my abortion experience] all the time. Otherwise, I let others talk about my experience for me." Her story is a powerful testimony of how abortion is a blessing. She wrote in a piece for Blavity, "My journey to have an abortion and care for myself strengthened my relationship with God and showed me how personal and intimate religion truly is. From my faith and my abortion, I know firsthand that abortion is a blessing. It is a blessing for parents, families and all people. And I know the life I love so much today—a life where I am more deeply connected to my family, my community and my God than ever—would have been impossible without it."[11] The decision to have an abortion is a sacred choice. For young people in particular, it is often a marker of their growing up, of claiming ownership and responsibility for their lives and futures. Abortion access is essential for young people. Without it, Lori, Veronika, CoWanda, and so many others would never have had the opportunity to pursue their dreams and callings of helping others find healing.

Laws that restrict abortion access for young people assume that they lack the capacity to make a sound, informed decision on their own. Parental notification and consent laws are unjust and out of touch with the reality that many young people have had to navigate their own survival long before they needed an abortion. We need to bring an end to these dehumanizing practices that require far too many young people to beg to have their reproductive freedom recognized by a judge. The decision of when to become a parent is a sacred one, and young people deserve better than having their fate left in the hands of adult strangers in courtrooms.

6

FOR A JUST SOCIETY

> For I am about to create new heavens and a new earth; the former
> things shall not be remembered or come to mind.
>
> —Isaiah 65:17

When we pursue justice and compassion, I believe we are cocreating heaven on earth with God. As we work to identify, confront, and dismantle interlocking systems of oppression, we transform the conditions that make life a living hell for so many people. Like the process of untangling a complicated knot, striving for social change is not glamorous, nor is it immediately rewarding. It's frustrating! Sometimes our strategies are counterproductive to our mission. We end up reinforcing the very systems and ideologies that we set out to deconstruct. This is especially true when we are well intentioned yet ill informed.

I see this often in myself as I work to unlearn internalized racism and discover all of the ways that my whiteness has shaped me to center myself in justice work. Each time I have to stop, reexamine, learn, make amends, and start again. I have to let go of the idea that progress is linear.

What inspires us to continue, in spite of our mistakes and disappointments, is sharing a vision of what the world *could* be. So often our discussions around social change focus on the realities we seek to transform. What if we spent more time daring to imagine the possibilities of a new reality?

The prophet Isaiah models this type of bold theological imagination in Isaiah 65. He speaks to a traumatized people, who have endured invasion, destruction, and enslavement, about the glorious "new heavens and a new earth" that God is creating and will continue to create for them. They will be the center of God's rejoicing, delight, and blessing. They will live in peace, enjoy prosperity, and experience abundance for generations to come. Amid the glorious descriptions of this new creation, one line in particular stands out to me: "They shall not labor in vain, or bear children for calamity; for they shall be offspring blessed by the Lord—and their descendants as well" (Isaiah 65:23). This is God's promise of an end to the generational trauma of reproductive loss.

Years ago, a vision came to me: a world in which every positive pregnancy test would be cause for celebration. For some time, I kept it to myself because I feared the idea would be disregarded as too simplistic, too naive, and too far removed from our current reality. But eventually I worked up the nerve to share my dream with other advocates in the field. It isn't a perfect model by any stretch, but simply daring to imagine a different reality shifted the tone of the conversation to one that was hope filled and forward thinking. So many times, our lack of imagination, or our unwillingness to dream big, can close us off from hope and keep us stuck in the cycle of despair. When we release our fears and doubts, we open ourselves to divine possibilities, even the most far-fetched ones.

The work of social transformation is holding that bold vision in one hand while addressing what stands in the way of its enactment in the other. For example, if we want to create a world in which every positive pregnancy test is cause for celebration, we have to ask what that would require of us collectively in terms of resource allocation, systems of support, and spiritual leadership. In order to tackle the societal changes necessary for that idea to take shape, we have to start by being honest about where we are. Currently in the United States,

- nearly half of all pregnancies each year are unplanned;[1]
- maternal mortality is on the rise, particularly among Black, Indigenous, and other communities of color, and the rate has doubled over the last thirty years;[2]
- there is no national paid sick leave or caregiver leave policy;
- nearly one-third of single mothers and their children are living in poverty;[3]
- more than thirty-two million people, roughly 15 percent of the population, have no health insurance coverage;[4]
- our public spending on programs to support families, including childcare, ranks close to the bottom among wealthy nations.[5]

I could fill this entire chapter with statistics that illustrate how little regard we have for the lives of pregnant people, parents, children, and families in our society. Women of color have been pointing this out for decades. Their critique of the mostly white-led reproductive rights movement is spot on: by narrowly focusing on the right to abortion, the movement centered the needs of wealthy white communities at the expense of everyone else's. The historic and systematic reproductive oppression of communities of color has taken many forms: sterilization without consent, contraceptive coercion, shackling during childbirth, forced surrogacy, family separation, denial of adoption services to LGBTQ+ individuals, environmental devastation, police violence, and on and on. Ensuring access to abortion alone has never been sufficient to achieve reproductive freedom and dignity for marginalized communities.

To address the holistic needs and concerns of their communities, women of color organized and created comprehensive, inclusive frameworks to address these myriad injustices. In 1990, the Native American Women's Health Education Resource Center (NAWHERC) and the Religious Coalition for Abortion Rights cosponsored a meeting of Indigenous women from eleven nations to develop the "Agenda for Native Women's Reproductive Justice," which called for a holistic approach to reproductive rights that included access to culturally competent sexuality education and health care as well as the right to parent in an environment free of racism and sexism.[6] Four years later, a group of twelve Black women gathered to create their human rights–based reproductive justice framework, which asserts the right to have children, the right not to have children, and the right to raise children in safe, healthy environments. In *Undivided Rights: Women of Color Organizing for Reproductive Justice*, the authors describe reproductive justice as "a theory, a practice, and a strategy . . . [that] defines the complicated, intersectional injuries endured and enables the re-envisioning of collective futures."[7] Activists in the reproductive justice movement today continue to advocate for this holistic approach, daring to imagine a vastly different world and building it piece by piece.

As we make space for grief, we ought to include the grief that comes from living in a society that does not support the reproductive decisions people make, no matter what those are. There is grief in reckoning with the way that our stated societal values impact the ways we allocate resources and provide services. The stories in this chapter challenge us to discern what values we want to embody, not just in our rhetoric, but also in our actions individually and collectively. What might be possible that we have not yet seen?

Alex (Name Changed), Texas

"I feel this pressure as a storyteller not to talk about my complicated feelings. It's so easy to take something out of context, weaponize it, and say, 'This person regrets their abortion.' But I do have feelings about it. I just don't want those feelings I have used to deny other people their abortions."

While most of the people I spoke with never thought that they would need an abortion, Alex never expected to become pregnant in the first place. Alex, who identifies as nonbinary transgender and uses they/them pronouns, is married to a trans woman. Prior to their wife's transition surgery, she was told by the doctor who managed her hormone treatment that because she had been on estrogen for so long, she was sterile. "That ended up being inaccurate," Alex said. "We have bad information as far as the fertility of trans people goes." Currently, there is simply not enough research dedicated to understanding the impact of hormone therapy and other treatments on the future fertility of trans people. In a survey of health providers who provide trans health care, doctors reported "a high level of clinical uncertainty" regarding their patients' reproductive health.[8]

As two trans people, Alex and their wife never imagined the possibility of having biological children together. They had a loving, supportive, and established relationship. They were deeply devoted to one another and committed to building a lifelong partnership together. Having a child could bring them even closer together. But practically, they were not in a position to become parents. At the time of their pregnancy, Alex was unemployed. They were applying for jobs, and while technically, employers cannot discriminate against pregnant people, it still happens all the time.[9]

Physically and psychologically, the pregnancy was a horrible experience from the start. Even prior to taking a pregnancy test, Alex was hit with a wave of fatigue and depression so debilitating they couldn't get out of bed for three days. "There was no way I could've held down a job feeling like that. I was so sick and dizzy that I was afraid to go anywhere. Being pregnant was not livable by any stretch. It was just not something I had the capacity to deal with," they told me. They needed to terminate the pregnancy.

Alex and their wife live in Texas, a state that requires the clinic technician to describe the ultrasound to the pregnant person. That was when, at six weeks pregnant, Alex learned that they were pregnant with twins. "That was a shock," they said. Texas also requires people to wait twenty-four hours after the first appointment before getting an abortion. Having that time to think only solidified Alex's decision. But at the same time, they were thinking about how special twins are. "In a theoretical sense, it felt amazing to think about raising twins, but realistically, we were not in a position to parent two children," they said. "The US does not have a welfare state. There's no universal health care or robust assistance for people who find themselves pregnant unexpectedly."

Our conversation took an interesting turn when Alex brought up the issue of adoption, which was the only time an interviewee brought this up. They said, "I'm not against adoption. But I know from my research, adoption can cause a lot of trauma to birth parents and adopted children." Alex and their wife are both white, and they feared that two "perfect white babies" would be seen as the "adoption jackpot" while other children of other races, ages, and abilities were overlooked. "I knew my children would benefit from racial inequalities, and it made me sick to think of them living with a family that would value them more because of their whiteness," they commented. Alex also worried about the likelihood that genetically, their children would identify as queer, have a disability like a mental illness, or both—and that they might be raised by families who would not accept them as they grew up. "I wouldn't have been able to protect them from people who would objectify them based on their desirability as white infant twins and then later reject them if they didn't measure up to that ideal—like if they were queer or mentally ill like their biological parents," they shared.

Alex said, "These twins are a figment of my imagination. I loved them for being part of me and my wife. I loved the children they would have become. But I chose not to allow them to become children. I'm OK with that. There are some complicated feelings there, but I don't spend a lot of time dwelling on them." Even in speaking these words, Alex is acutely aware of how these thoughts and ideas could be tokenized and weaponized against abortion access. Their mission is to normalize people having abortions, to reframe the issue as one that impacts more than cisgender women, and to send the message that their life is better because they had an abortion: "I want people seeking abortion care to know that they are supported and loved by a community larger than they could ever imagine."

When Alex woke up from the abortion, they were relieved not to be pregnant anymore. Even though that ended up being their only chance at biological parenting—Alex's wife had transition surgery a few months later—Alex is certain that it was the right choice. "I was so desperate not to be pregnant," they told me. "Abortion saved my life."

Erin Outson, St. Louis, Missouri

> "I don't regret my choice at all. It was a big decision, and I live forever connected to the grief of having to decide to be or not to be a parent. But the gift of abortion was it taught me how to make a decision exactly for me that no one else could have ever made."

Erin and I connected when we worked for the same faith-based advocacy office in Washington, DC. Our paths crossed just before she made plans to move to Chicago, and I had my eye on life back in

North Carolina. The week before she moved, I passed along to her my ankle-length puffer jacket that I'd worn during the long, cold winters of Connecticut while I was in seminary. Even though our time working together was short, she was a kindred spirit, and we stayed connected, exchanging email updates from time to time. In 2019, Erin reached out to me about her abortion experience and her desire to get involved with faith-based organizations working on reproductive freedom. When I started this book project, she was one of the first people I approached about doing an interview. Graciously, she agreed.

It was 2018. Erin had been living as an artist in Chicago when she decided to move to St. Louis and enroll in seminary. When she began a new chapter of her life in this new city, she already had mastered the wearing of a "ministerial mask": she compartmentalized and performed the part of a spiritual leader, only revealing to her seminary classmates the parts of herself she deemed befitting of someone serious about ministry. Underneath that, though, was a much more complex reality. She was living a double life.

Soon after she started graduate school, Erin started seeing a powerful man in the community, a high school principal who was well regarded for his leadership both in education and in social justice causes. What presumably no one knew was that he was an abuser and a narcissist. Erin never thought she would find herself in a relationship like this. "It was part of this trope of being a middle-class white woman," she said. "I was not supposed to be vulnerable to this kind of relationship." When Erin discovered she was pregnant, he abandoned her, and she felt she had no recourse, given his position in the community. "No one would believe me," she said.

Once again, Erin had to reckon with a reality that she never imagined for her life: she was pregnant, uninsured, and alone. As she weighed her options, she struggled with the messages she had gotten about sexuality, abortion, and embodiment growing up. Her parents were supportive of legal abortion, but there was a clear delineation between those who needed abortion—people "out there"—and those who did not. The message from her white liberal Christian family was implicit but understood: abortion was not something she should ever need.

Erin seriously considered single parenting and began to research available resources. As an uninsured full-time student, Erin had to fight to get basic medical services, like prenatal care, and she had the realization that this would be her life: constantly battling for what she needed. She knew that her whiteness afforded her privilege, and even for her, navigating the system was next to impossible. "There is a difference between choice and access," she said.

What she lacked in financial support she had in social support. She confided in trusted friends and loved ones who pledged to stand by her, no matter what path she chose. But they were honest about their concerns too. Support for low-income families in the United States is practically nonexistent. "If I had been living in another country, if I had been in a place where community and structural resources were equitable, we might have been having different conversations," she reflected. "I knew that I could be a single parent, but it was going to be incredibly hard."

After talking with her friends, Erin still wasn't sure what she wanted to do. She turned inward and asked herself what it was that *she* wanted. What emerged was the clarity that this was not her time to be a parent. "I didn't want to give birth to my ancestor's pains. This was not going to be my story as it had been for so many before me," she said. She made an appointment at Hope Clinic for a medication abortion, a procedure some had described to her as equivalent to the discomfort of a teeth cleaning. But for Erin, the pain was awful and so intense that she passed out. She was home alone throughout the whole ordeal. "People don't know how to support you when you're having an abortion," she told me. "I had a big fight with my family about it. How is it that when someone is having knee surgery, people come to support them, but they didn't think to support me during my abortion?"

A week later, Erin went in for a follow-up appointment, including an ultrasound. After scanning her uterus, the ultrasound technician gave her the news: "I'm so sorry. You're still pregnant." The medication had not worked properly, and she would need a surgical abortion. Erin felt devastated and alone: "This woman who gave me the news got to leave, and I was still pregnant." A nurse came in to schedule the procedure, but Erin was overwhelmed with emotion and left the clinic before making an appointment. She got into her car and thought to herself, *I can't go through another abortion.*

From the parking lot of the clinic, she called and asked to speak with the doctor. Erin asked her if continuing the pregnancy would be possible. Her doctor was kind and supportive. She would make a referral to another clinic, and in the meantime, she would pass along all the research and journal articles she could find on failed medication abortions. But a week later, Erin began to bleed. She was having a miscarriage. "The decision was made for me," Erin recounted. She returned to the clinic for a D&C (dilation and curettage) to remove the remaining tissue.

When she got home, Erin thought about her pregnancy and all of the circumstances surrounding it. Underneath the entire ordeal, she saw unprocessed trauma that she needed to address. She asked herself, *Who do I want to be in this world? What am I willing to suffer through, and for what am I no longer willing to suffer?* She realized that she had the power to determine the trajectory of her life. Her abortion was, as she described it, "the transformational moment I needed for my life." But there was grief too—deep and complicated grief. Most of the time it showed up as anger that the world was not as it should be, that it was not set up for pregnant people to make actual choices for their lives. "I'm meant to be a mother," she lamented. But she also knew that having a child with her abuser would have continued a line of ancestral pain from those before her who had not been able to determine when and with whom they would parent. She was adamant about bringing an end to that pattern.

Erin and I spent a lot of time talking about her pathway to healing. The process has been about much more than her abortion. Reclaiming her body and listening to her inner voice have been essential. She has reconnected parts of herself through ritual and art. When she feels detached from her body, she turns to movement practices that ground her physically. As she continues down this path of self-discovery, she hopes to help guide others to explore their stories and find healing. This is her ministry, as she describes it, of "building landscapes in the desert geography, a place where there has not been enough attention, water, and soil—and not enough love."

Erin is starting right where she is in her seminary environment. "Abortion was the gateway to understanding how institutions in general, but specifically seminaries—deep places of soul work supposedly—are not set up for a whole person," she said. She looks for opportunities to share her story with her classmates. When the seminary hired a new dean of students, Erin made an appointment to advocate for more support and discussion on campus about reproductive justice. Being this outspoken about her abortion has required a lot of inner work. "When people make decisions that are going to be shamed at best and hated at worst, you have to get clear about who you are before you show up in a room and talk about it," she explained. "But when I tell my story, I know others can tell their stories. That's the only way we have healing."

Months after our interview, Erin shared these thoughts with me, which sum up the beautiful complexity of her abortion experience:

> Abortion and all its intersections changed me for the better. People think it's the choice that changes you, but it's what it connects you to. I would have never understood race, class, and patriarchy in the way I do now if it wasn't for abortion. I would never have understood whiteness and privilege. And I would have never found my life's work: that abortion be made public, as it serves the healing and education of our collective for the better because it intersects with everything—with sex, bodies, relationships, joy, the welfare of children, sovereignty—all the things. So abortion is the gift, and the choice was a necessary portal into choosing to listen to my soul for the first time.

Kim Jorgensen Gane, St. Joseph, Michigan

> "I couldn't possibly have fallen farther off the 'perfect, pure Michigan' white girl pedestal."

On December 1, 1986, Kim was driving when she heard the shocking news that the Planned Parenthood clinic in Kalamazoo, Michigan, had been firebombed. She pulled the car over to the side of the road in order to collect herself. The year before, she'd had an abortion at that very clinic, and she was now pregnant again. Her only thought was, *Thank God no one has to know.*

Thirty years later, Kim sat in an auditorium to watch a student-led production called the *Pro Voice Monologues*, a show about abortion storytelling. Afterward there was a panel discussion with a representative from Planned Parenthood, an elected official, and to her surprise, a minister. *He's going to be on the other side*, Kim thought. *I'm going to be judged for having an abortion.*

"Nowhere in Scripture is abortion condemned," she heard the pastor say. Kim struggled to hold back tears. "I knew I had internalized stories from the Bible, like how I was taught that Eve ruined everything, but I didn't realize how much that informed how I felt about myself," she said.

As a young girl, she had spent her Sunday mornings in the front pew of the church where her grandmother had served as the choir director. She absorbed the teachings about women she heard from the pulpit—that women were temptresses and little else—and understood that simply having a female body was sinful. When Kim was a teenager, she was sexually assaulted. Those messages about women and sin haunted her. They made her believe that no matter what happened to her, it was always somehow her fault. The shame of having been raped shut her down and kept her quiet. She told no one.

In 1985, Kim was training for a new job in Kalamazoo when she discovered she was pregnant. She knew she needed an abortion, but she knew she couldn't go to her family for help. In the end, she told only three people about her decision: the man who'd gotten her pregnant, a coworker, and her new roommate. Even though they barely knew each other, Kim's roommate took her to the clinic. Two years later, she attended Kim's baby shower.

When Kim discovered she was pregnant for a second time, she said, "I couldn't face the shame of another abortion. I procrastinated to the point that I had no choice but to go through with the pregnancy." During the first six months, she worked three jobs and struggled to make ends meet. She hid the pregnancy for as long as she could, but eventually she had to move back in with her mother. Kim's parents had divorced when she was in high school, and her mother lived with an abusive boyfriend, prone to fits of rage that sometimes became physically violent. Kim remembers seeing bruises on her mother's arms after a fight. A few months later she gave birth to a baby girl, and not long after that, her mother got pregnant with Kim's half brother. With three adults, two babies, and a few pets running around the tiny 1,200-square-foot house they shared, Kim knew she had to find a way out of there. She managed to save up some money from babysitting, and when her daughter was a toddler, Kim moved them into their own tiny apartment. It wasn't much, but it was theirs.

Single parenting was incredibly difficult, financially and emotionally. Kim shared that in 1984, the year before her abortion and three years before the birth of her daughter, she had cast her first vote for Ronald Reagan ("because that's who my dad was voting for," she told me), whose platform included opposition to abortion in all circumstances. President Reagan had railed against the "welfare queens," a racist and inaccurate stereotype of poor single mothers, usually Black women, who allegedly abused social support programs to avoid employment. Reagan promoted this racist, classist myth to justify his slashing of social support programs.

Kim had terminated a pregnancy and carried one to term, and she felt like she could not win. "Like many other single moms, I worked multiple jobs, went without, and did everything I could to avoid asking for or needing help of any kind because of these myths," she said. "As far as society goes, I couldn't make a 'right' choice. No matter what, it was the 'wrong' choice." She desperately wanted to avoid the shame of fitting into this "welfare queen" stereotype, no matter the costs. There were times when she had to skip meals, choose which bills to pay that month, and write bad checks. The isolation and stress were overwhelming. "I didn't want to ask for help because of the guilt and shame I felt," she said. "I wanted to be self-sufficient, but the reality was much harder."

The stress of trying to make ends meet and care for her daughter on her own was isolating. In a piece she wrote for a show called *Listen to Your Mother*, Kim described the feeling as "a cavernous loneliness from working and earning never enough; from returning bottles and cans from my dad's office for their 5-cent deposit to buy bread and milk and eggs to feed my little girl; from raiding my dad's change jar for quarters to go to the Laundromat to wash our clothes."[10] Kim became depressed to the point that she thought about ending her life.

When I asked her if she ever sought help for her depression, she said no. She told no one. The shame kept her quiet.

Somehow Kim managed to survive those early years of single parenting in poverty. As difficult as her situation was, Kim recognizes the privileges she had that helped her make it through those times: her whiteness, her excellent public school education, and the opportunities of a well-connected family. At every turn, even if she felt like she couldn't ask for it, there were people to help her, from finding an apartment she could mostly afford to eventually securing better-paying employment that got her financially stable. Several years later, Kim met and married her husband, a single father of a daughter just two years younger than her own and a former firefighter, paramedic, and police officer. (Interestingly, she would learn later that he had been a first responder to the scene of the Planned Parenthood bombing in 1986.)

Though her abortion was decades ago, Kim's healing process is ongoing. When she and her husband decided to have a child together, they struggled with infertility for six years and experienced a miscarriage before giving birth to their son. Like many who struggle with infertility, even those who have never terminated a pregnancy, Kim felt enormous shame and guilt about her inability to conceive. Again, those biblical messages of women "being fruitful" and the self-blaming thoughts of what she might have done to deserve this infertility filled her mind. She felt the same kind of loneliness in that experience as she had during her abortion and the early years of single parenthood.

Today Kim is working to break the isolation that so many people feel at these critical moments in their reproductive lives, no matter what decisions they make. She writes and speaks about her complicated experiences with parenthood publicly, including as a national storyteller with Planned Parenthood. In a speech she gave in 2018, she said, "I am a mother by choice. But motherhood is complicated. Before we gave birth to you, believe it or not, we were fully formed human beings with hopes and dreams and futures of our own. And for me that time includes an abortion story too. I believe that telling my story is divine work. I am not ashamed."

One of the things I often say is "Resist simple answers to life's complex questions." There is so much nuance in each of these experiences and in nearly every abortion story I have ever heard. In their own ways, Kim, Erin, and Alex point to the ways that we collectively fail to support people in their reproductive decisions by abandoning them at their time of need, by refusing to fund programs that help low-income families, and by ignoring our responsibility to care for one another. As reproductive justice advocates have pointed out again and again, there can be no actual choice if one does not have access to what is needed to make a decision and to thrive.

Can we dare to imagine what would happen if we embodied family values by implementing adequate structures and programs to support parents and children? Can we expand our theological imagination and shift our public discourse toward an orientation of compassion instead of judgment? What a world that would be.

7

FOR THE GOOD OF GROWTH

We know that all things work together for good for those who love God.

—Romans 8:28

Abortion is a blessing.

If that sentence made you uncomfortable, I understand. Abortion stigma impacts all of us, myself included. Let me explain what I mean when I say that abortion is a blessing. I am not claiming that abortion is easy or without loss, grief, or other complicated emotions. To the contrary, I am affirming that the very process of identifying and coming to terms with one's full experience of abortion can lead to tremendous growth and positive change in a person's life. Abortion has the power not only to save lives but to bless them too.

As I talked with people about their experiences, I heard about the ways that abortion helped wake them up to the realities of their lives that they might have ignored otherwise. By making the decision to end a pregnancy, they gained clarity about their sense of purpose and direction in the world. Some ended relationships that were abusive, toxic, or otherwise unfulfilling. Others spent time exploring their desires to become parents or not in the future. Many say that having an abortion helped them turn inward and uncover truths hidden within themselves.

Take a moment to bring to mind some of the times in your own life when you experienced significant personal growth. My guess is that it was not during a time of calm and peace. It was likely a time of chaos, grief, confusion, or uncertainty.

One of these times in my life happened just a few years ago when I was in the middle of some sudden professional upheaval. Even though these changes were mostly positive, at least from the outside, I was surprised by how my emotions were all over the place, ranging from sadness and anger to self-doubt and anxiety. With all of this negative emotional energy swirling around me, I began to wonder if I had made a mistake by making this decision to take on a new endeavor. If it was a good decision, why was it making me feel so bad?

At the recommendation of a few friends, I picked up a copy of the book *Transitions: Making Sense of Life's Changes* with the hope that it would help me work through my confusing feelings. Author William Bridges describes the difference between a change and a transition. A change can be a decision we make or a thing that happens, but a transition is an internal process of coming to terms with the change. It requires us to go inward, to let go of the past, and to come to a place of acceptance of a new reality. Every change is an ending of something. The transition of coming to terms with that ending is where our growth happens, and oftentimes it involves loss.

So much of our public conversations and debates on abortion focus on the moment of decision and the moment of access. Particularly in pro-choice circles, we pay little attention to the ways that someone processes their abortion, how they weave it into the greater narrative arc of their lives. In other words, we ignore the ways that people make meaning of their abortion experiences.

As an adolescent, I was taught a simplistic faith in God's good plans for my life. If you grew up in a white evangelical church like I did, you may have been encouraged to memorize this verse (completely out of its historical context) from Jeremiah: "For surely I know the plans I have for you, says the Lord, plans for your welfare and not for harm, to give you a future with hope" (Jeremiah 29:11). My idea of what those divine plans were exactly was sophomoric; I was a teenager after all. But putting childish things aside, the basic sentiment of releasing my anxieties about the future and putting my trust in Spirit to work things out remains a central part of my faith today. When I feel out of control and I'm grasping for answers, I return to the practice of surrendering to the unknown with the absolute knowing that somehow there are divine plans in the works that are orchestrated for my growth and my good. Even if the current circumstances are causing me pain, I believe that "all things work together for good" in the end (Romans 8:28).

The three stories in this chapter are filled with pain and joy, grief and growth. What ties them together is a shared commitment to caring for others who have abortions and offering them the loving, nonjudgmental support that they wish they'd had. Together these incredible women are shifting the culture of abortion one compassionate conversation at a time.

Adriana, New York, New York

> "After I had an abortion, it sparked so much change in my life. It made me stop and take inventory of everything happening in my life. I felt so out of control. It made me go inward and try to figure out what I wanted my life to look like. A lot of my healing has been taking active steps toward that."

Adriana was on a two-week work trip in New York City when she started having what felt like severe PMS symptoms. Her face had broken out, and her breasts were sore. At first, she was too caught up in the busyness of her trip to realize that her period was late. Later when she took a pregnancy test and it was positive, she felt like the ground had been ripped out from under her. "I could see my future chosen for me should I go through with the pregnancy," she recounted. She cut her trip short and booked a flight back home to San Francisco. Before boarding the plane, Adriana knew what she would do. When she got home, she would call to schedule an abortion as soon as possible.

Picturing that six-hour trip home, I asked what was going through her head during the flight. She said that she felt relief that abortion was an option for her, that she didn't have to continue the pregnancy, and that this moment wasn't going to determine her future. She also felt guilty by how relieved she felt. She wondered if she was supposed to be feeling worse about her decision. Over the next several months,

Adriana would cycle through a range of emotions: relief, guilt, sadness, and shame. Sometimes these tough feelings would creep out of nowhere and surprise her. But of course, the healing process is never as linear as we would like it to be. "Just because abortion is common doesn't mean it's easy to go through," she said.

Adriana talked about the messages she got about sexuality as a child. She and her sister grew up in a culturally Catholic family with parents who had immigrated to the United States from El Salvador when they were in their twenties. When they had their daughters, they enrolled them in Catholic school, where the message about sex was clear: sex for pleasure was dirty, and only procreative sex within marriage was acceptable. At home, there wasn't much conversation about sex at all. In her household, she said the unspoken rule was "You don't talk about sex, because it doesn't exist." But she does remember an odd explanation her mother gave her about where babies came from, an anecdote that would later become a family joke: when you get married, the priest asks if you want to have a baby. If you say yes, he gives you a seed that you swallow, and that's how the baby grows. Adriana laughed as she told me about going to school and repeating this to her classmates, insistent that it was true. Later, when Adriana was in high school and dating her first serious boyfriend, her mother did mention birth control briefly, and she also informed Adriana that if she got pregnant, having an abortion "would not be a choice" because "it's a sin," and their family would work together to help raise her child. Adriana shared that her mother had been pregnant and unmarried, which had been difficult. Understandably, Adriana has never shared about her decision to have an abortion with her parents.

Thankfully, Adriana had other support. She confided in a friend who'd had an abortion years earlier and her sister, who initially was shocked when she learned about the pregnancy but then went on to help Adriana navigate the health care end of things, doing research on abortion providers and collecting information regarding options. Compared to many, Adriana had quite a bit of support, yet she still felt completely isolated. She reflected, "I had what you'd consider 'support'—my best friend, only sister, and partner were present and there for me. I had the resources, money, and access to the care I needed. If that was my experience and I still felt isolated and alone—how must others feel who don't have anyone? How can we be failing people over a clear health matter?" There is so much to be done in providing holistic care and resources for people who have abortions. As Adriana researched her options, she kept stumbling across websites and online forums that disguised themselves as supportive of all reproductive decisions but were sponsored by antiabortion Christian ministries. The posts were full of misinformation about abortion. "I couldn't trust those stories," she said.

The time between Adriana discovering her pregnancy and having her abortion was around two weeks. She went to the University of California San Francisco hospital, where the process was straightforward, and she felt welcomed and cared for by the staff. They explained all of her options and asked how she was doing emotionally with her decision to end the pregnancy. As Adriana described it, "They were very normalizing of the experience but also supportive in not minimizing it." This reflected my own experience volunteering in a clinic that offered abortion. In the end, Adriana opted for the medication abortion and went home. The abortion process was physically painful.

Adriana's cramps were intense and lasted several days. Her partner was with her, but he didn't know how to care for her through this. She felt like she was going through the experience completely on her own.

After her abortion, Adriana embarked on an inner journey of soul searching and healing. She wanted clarity about the direction of her life. Now that she had made this decision to end her pregnancy, she wanted to make something of her life so that when she looked back, she would see that that choice had been worth the pain. She began to make major changes: she quit her job, moved to New York, and trained to be a doula.

Today Adriana continues to find healing by helping others. She volunteers for Exhale, an organization that provides nonjudgmental afterabortion emotional support and offers loving support to those who need it. She reflected, "It's been so healing to normalize the conversation around abortion and talk with people who have had the same experience, though each story is unique and different. Helping others has helped me come to acceptance of my own experience." While there is still so much work to be done in providing support to people who have abortions, she is grateful to play her small part in helping others feel less alone.

Ashley, Boston, Massachusetts

> "For my whole life, I thought I believed in abortion for other people, but I would never do it. And then I did."

Ashley had just turned twenty-four when she started dating a former coworker seventeen years her senior. They'd only been together a few months when he invited her to France. As soon as they arrived, though, she began to question their relationship. "We were in such different stages of life," she told me. She decided to break it off. A few days later, she discovered that she was pregnant. She called him to figure out what to do, and he promised to support whatever decision she made.

Ashley vacillated. She made two appointments to have an abortion and didn't go either time. "I just wasn't ready to make that final choice," she said. The pregnancy *did* mean something to her, and she knew that he would make an amazing father. She began educating herself about pregnancy and childbirth.

As Ashley debated what to do, she reflected a lot on her own childhood. She'd grown up in a broken family. Her parents had separated for the final time when she was seven years old. "They had a rough relationship," she said. "I never want that for my children. It's absolutely OK to coparent with someone, but I didn't want to stay together for the kid." She couldn't see herself having a baby with someone who wouldn't be part of her life for the long term. She called the clinic a third time to make an appointment, and at seventeen weeks, Ashley had an abortion. "I'm grateful that I live in a time when I can decide when I want to be a parent," she shared.

A few weeks before that, she had a fainting spell and took herself to the emergency room to get checked out. Because they were running tests, she needed to disclose that she was pregnant. The hospital staff responded with heartfelt congratulations. "Are you going to give birth here?" they asked. They assumed that she was happy about the pregnancy. When they did an ultrasound, no one asked if she wanted to look at it; they just showed it to her. She captured a short video on her phone, a memory she still keeps.

Since Ashley was in her second trimester, before her procedure, she first needed to have her cervix dilated, a step that would set the abortion process in motion. Afterward she was given pain medication and told to go home. She would return the following day for the abortion. The cervical dilation had been the first step of her process, and the surgical procedure would complete it. The time between leaving the clinic and returning the next day was the hardest part for her. "I couldn't back out if I wanted to," she said. She just wanted the waiting to be over.

The next day, Ashley prepared herself for the protesters she would face. Even though there were supportive clinic escorts available to walk with her to the door, she didn't need them and calmly made her way inside unbothered by the protesters' yelling. Inside the clinic walls, Ashley felt nothing but kindness and compassion. The staff explained everything to her and assured her complete confidentiality. As she sat in the waiting room, she experienced a mixture of emotions. She saw people from all walks of life waiting right alongside her. "The statistics about abortion are right," she said. Until then she had felt like the stereotype of the "young irresponsible person who gets an abortion," as she put it. But seeing people of all ages and backgrounds there gave her a lot of comfort.

Reflecting on her abortion experience now, Ashley knows how privileged and fortunate she was to live in Massachusetts, where there aren't the kind of restrictions and barriers people face elsewhere. "I wasn't forced to look at an ultrasound and sit with that for days before having access to a procedure," she said. "I didn't have to travel to another state." For months after her abortion, Ashley waited for the day when a bill would arrive in the mail, but it never did. Eventually, she looked up the details of her insurance coverage, and she was surprised and grateful to learn that abortion was covered. "When I learned that it was taken care of, there was almost an equal weight lifted off my chest," she told me. She was barely making ends meet, living paycheck to paycheck in a shared house with roommates at the time. Having to pay for an expensive medical procedure would have been incredibly difficult.

While the logistics of the abortion were simple to navigate, the emotional part of her journey was difficult. Other than her former partner, Ashley told no one about her abortion. "I felt like I was carrying this deep, dark secret," she told me. Shortly after the abortion, her best friend got pregnant. Even though they were close, Ashley didn't feel like she could be forthcoming about her own pregnancy. She watched her friend become a parent, all the while wondering what might have been.

Not long after her abortion, Ashley's father died after a tragic car accident. The grieving process was painful, but it made her more compassionate toward anyone going through a loss. She took classes about bereavement and realized how often we encounter hurting people without any idea of what they are going through. Years later, when a coworker got pregnant and needed an abortion, Ashley finally decided to share her story. She could see that this woman needed someone to say, "Me too. I've been there." When she realized how much it helped when she shared, she started being more open about it with people when it felt right to do so. The more people she told, the more people opened up about their own abortion stories. She joined a Facebook support group for people going through abortion experiences, not so much for her to share her own story, but to support others. She also volunteers with Exhale. "The biggest thing that heals me is helping other people through similar experiences," she told me.

Ashley knows that she would not be the empathetic and caring person she is today were it not for her abortion. She hopes to change the narrative for people like her who experience abortion as a loss, knowing now how beauty and grief often go hand in hand. Ashley, who is now a trained birth doula, shared about the first time she witnessed a birth. She likened that experience to the passing of her father. "I've seen death, and now I've seen birth," she said. The two are inextricably linked. There are times when she feels sad about her pregnancy, but she knows that is just how grief works.

"I don't need to make it go away," she said. "Just like the loss of my father, my abortion will always be there. I will always be sad about it, and that's OK."

Jocelyn, San Francisco, California

> "I didn't touch you, but I felt you. I didn't know you, but I loved you. I loved you, my first, my only."

Imagine this sequence of events. First, you learn you've earned a coveted spot in a teacher training program. You're absolutely elated because this has been a dream for years. The next day, you receive even more life-changing news: you have been accepted into a graduate program in education. You feel like you're on top of the world. Then, the following day, you wake up early to get ready for work, and when you come downstairs, you find your boyfriend of five years drunk on the couch and smoking cigarettes at six in the morning. You're beyond fed up, and as much as you love him, you tell him he has to leave. The relationship is over. A few hours later, you take a pregnancy test, a routine measure for someone with an irregular menstrual cycle. For the first time, it's positive. You call the boyfriend you just kicked out of your apartment and tell him that he needs to turn around and come back. The two of you need to talk.

This was Jocelyn's complicated life in 2015. She told me the whole story over the phone while she was on a hike near her home in San Francisco. "I'd rather not have my roommates hear me," she said. At the time of her pregnancy, Jocelyn was working in the toddler classroom at a local preschool. She loved her job, but she had dreams of becoming a certified teacher. Now the opportunity was right in front of her. Everything that she'd worked so hard for was at her fingertips. But she was pregnant. There was no chance of a long-term future with her partner, even though they loved each other. He was an alcoholic who struggled with depression and couldn't hold down a job.

Jocelyn did not want to have an abortion. She loves children and has wanted to be a mother for as long as she can remember. Having an abortion was something that she simply needed to do. In the preschool bathroom, she made the call to Planned Parenthood to schedule a medication abortion. Ten days later, on the morning of her appointment, she was a wreck. Everyone at the clinic told her that she didn't have to do this now, that she could come back another day if and when she felt better about her decision. Jocelyn knew that if she left that day, she would never come back. She swallowed the dose of mifepristone and went home.

The abortion was excruciating. She was in so much pain that she thought something was wrong. She called the clinic, and they assured her that what was going on was within the wide range of normal. They told her to expect heavy bleeding for a couple of days, and after that, it should taper off. But five weeks after she'd taken the pills, Jocelyn was still bleeding. "It was this constant reminder of what I had done," she said. She went in for a follow-up appointment at the clinic, where they did an ultrasound, which showed that her uterine lining was a little thicker than it should be, but they were confident that it would resolve on its own. If the bleeding continued longer than a week, she should come back and get checked out again.

The day after that follow-up appointment, Jocelyn was in the shower when she started to pass large blood clots. She was bleeding so heavily that she had to change her tampon every ten minutes. Scared and unsure of what to do, she called the clinic about what was happening, and they urged her to go to the emergency room immediately. By the time she arrived at the University of San Francisco hospital, her pants were soaked in blood down to the knees.

The doctors ran a series of tests and concluded that she was among the 1 percent of people who have a rare complication after taking mifepristone. Her cervix had not dilated enough to pass the tissue completely, so her body was continuing to send blood to the uterus as if the pregnancy were continuing normally. This was why she was hemorrhaging. They treated her immediate symptoms and slowed the bleeding, but when they suggested that she take another round of mifepristone, she adamantly refused. She was not about to go through that ordeal again. She wanted a surgical abortion, but the hospital could not provide her one that day. If she wanted a surgical procedure, she would have to go to another campus.

I was confused as to why the hospital, a major medical facility in a city like San Francisco, could not have treated her that day. The surgical procedure Jocelyn needed is common and uncomplicated, one that many people need in the wake of a miscarriage as well. Why did they not have the equipment to provide her one there that day? This speaks volumes about the state of reproductive health care in this country and the lack of access to care even when a person is in desperate need of medical attention.

Jocelyn fought with her insurance company over the need for a surgical abortion. She actually had to delay the date of her procedure because she wasn't sure it would be covered. The insurance company was arguing that a surgical procedure wasn't necessary because she had been offered a second dose of mifepristone, even though that was the medication that had led to her complications in the first place. Jocelyn lucked out: she spoke with a sympathetic employee who advocated for her, and in the end, the surgical procedure was covered. If she had spoken with another insurance agent that day, who knows what would have happened?

After the procedure, Jocelyn had to come to terms with everything that she had been through physically before she could begin healing emotionally. She continued to work at the preschool, and each morning as she watched parents drop off their little ones, she felt both a sense of guilt and longing. She worried what these parents would think of her if they knew that she'd been pregnant and then ended it.

I assured her that statistically, some of them had their own abortion experiences as well.

Similar to what Adriana shared with me, Jocelyn considers herself lucky to have had so much support in her life from her family and friends. Even with that circle of support, though, she found the entire abortion experience isolating. I could hear her choke up a little when she thought of all the people who have no one to turn to and how alone they must feel. We talked about all of the unnecessary suffering that people endure because of this isolation. That's why Jocelyn makes time to volunteer on the Exhale talk line. Helping others feel less alone is healing, even though being someone's support person can be difficult at times. Sometimes she doubts if she is making any difference at all, but then she remembers, "Every time I called the talk line, I felt helped. Hopefully that person feels helped too."

To help make peace with her decision, Jocelyn put together a box to honor her pregnancy. She included the pregnancy test, a sonogram picture, and a letter she wrote expressing appreciation and thanks for "this thing that was and this thing that wasn't." Jocelyn started making big changes in her life. She ended things with her boyfriend for good, and he entered a rehab program for his addiction. She enrolled in both the teacher training and the graduate program she had been accepted into days before she discovered her pregnancy. Rather than getting pulled into feelings of guilt and shame, she actively chooses to feel gratitude because of the positive changes she has made in her life since her abortion. Jocelyn plans to continue talking about her experience and helping others going through something similar. "It brings me into a community of people who know what having an abortion feels like, and I no longer feel alone," she told me.

Throughout our sacred texts, we receive the divine promise that we are never alone, that God is always with us. As human beings, we share a basic need to be seen, known, heard, and held in love. No one should have to go through an abortion alone, but the fear of judgment and shame keeps many from reaching out for what they need. Even when friends and family appear supportive, they often don't know what to say or do to help.

A good friend whose mother died unexpectedly years ago shared with me that part of the grieving process was having some of her dearest friends pull away emotionally while others unexpectedly stepped in to offer their love and support. They weren't her closest friends, but they knew grief intimately. They understood what it felt like to lose someone. The women in this chapter know the pain of isolation and secrecy, and they have made a conscious decision to draw strength from their experiences and offer the love and care that they wish they'd had. Because of their willingness to heal and grow, others don't have to feel so alone.

8

FOR COMMUNITIES THAT HEAL

Above all, clothe yourselves with love, which binds everything together in perfect harmony.

—Colossians 3:14

When the idea for this project came to me, we were about three months into the COVID-19 pandemic. The novelty of staying home had fully worn off, and the collective feeling of isolation had settled in to stay for the foreseeable future. Perhaps my own experience of disconnection made me even more sensitive to the loneliness I heard in the interviews. Nearly every person I interviewed, regardless of their circumstances, said they felt isolated at some point during the process. They shared a sense of having to go through it all on their own. Many shared the losses of relationships with friends and partners, distance from family members, and the ongoing tension of keeping secrets from loved ones. My heart broke as I imagined these vibrant, power-ful, and strong people having no one to turn to with their struggles.

This feeling of disconnection, which stems from the invalidation of our loss, is the cornerstone of disenfranchised grief. It's not unique to abortion. The same is true for those who experience infertility and miscarriage as well as those who make decisions to parent alone, to choose adoption, and to remain child-free. That's because the narrowly prescribed rules of our society regarding the creation of our families leave many of us outside the bounds of what is deemed desirable, or even acceptable. We feel abandoned by the people who claim to love us but judge us instead.

Our experiences with community, like abortion, are complex. There may be times when we feel both included and excluded in differ-ent ways. Eventually, we must ask ourselves, Do we stay or do we go? Sometimes the harm done is irreparable, and our only option is to leave. Any time we sever ties, even if we do it for our own self-preservation, there is loss. As imperfect as our relationships and com-munities are, no matter how many times they have failed us, we long to belong. The question is, Where and with whom?

This final chapter explores what it's like to be someone in a faith community who has had an abortion. The experiences range from deep hurt to deep healing, and sometimes they include both. They challenge us to examine the ways that our churches have caused harm and how we can work toward offering compassionate care in our sacred spaces.

Rev. Susan Chorley, Norwell, Massachusetts

"There's this hatred around regret. We give it too much power. I regret things all the time. I regret that I yelled at my son yesterday, and I'm working on myself so that hopefully I don't do it again today. But it doesn't change the fact that I did, in fact, do those things. The question isn't 'How do we live without regret?' but 'How do we make peace with it?'"

Have you met someone and had an inner knowing that the universe had gone out of its way to connect the two of you? Rev. Susan Chorley is one of those people for me. As we got to know each other, we uncovered so many connecting threads between us that I knew we were bound to find one another. We first met for coffee over the Thanksgiving holiday of 2017 while she was visiting family in North Carolina. I was at a point of searching in my life, and Susan was a pastor to me when I needed one.

I knew that Susan had an abortion story because of her work through Exhale—and because I'd read an interview that she had done for *Parents* magazine about mothers who have abortions. But it wasn't until I was preparing to write this book that she personally shared her story with me. Though all of the interviews I've done were sacred, this one felt especially so.

When Susan was a college student, she studied abroad for a semester in London. That was where she discovered that she was pregnant. Susan called her parents because she needed to tell them her boyfriend was going to deposit money into her account to pay for an abortion. Her father, a Baptist pastor, was the one who answered her call. When he picked up the phone, Susan said, "Dad, I need you to be my pastor right now." After hearing about her pregnancy and her plan to have an abortion, he assured Susan that he would support her and keep her confidentiality. When Susan's mother eventually found out, she had a harder time coping with the news, and her reaction was painful for Susan.

After the abortion, Susan finished up her semester in England and returned to North Carolina to complete her degree. Shortly after graduation, she moved to Seattle for a year of volunteer service and began exploring her path to ministry. She found a therapist and worked with a spiritual director assigned by her program. At first, she didn't realize that her spiritual director was a Catholic priest, but when she shared about her abortion, he responded compassionately and asked thoughtful questions. Finally, she had space to process what happened in England.

Ritual has always been important to Susan. She connected with a pastor who helped her create a personal ceremony of closure and healing around her abortion. Then Susan and her boyfriend decided to do something together, so they filled a bottle with messages along with a pair of baby booties and threw it into the ocean. They were twenty-two years old at the time. A few years later, they were married.

After the wedding, Susan and her husband moved to California, where she started seminary and gave birth to their son in her final semester. About two years later, Susan discovered that she was pregnant again. "I had always pictured having two children," she told me. But their marriage was starting to fall apart. She wasn't sure if they were going to be able to make their relationship work, and the last thing she wanted to do was bring another child into an unhealthy situation. She didn't think married people even had abortions. "I just assumed that when people are married, if you get pregnant, you have the kid," she told me. The reality is that 14 percent of all abortion patients are married, but I imagine that because of the shame and stigma, very few of them share this fact with their families and loved ones.[1]

In spite of her ambivalence and the feelings of judgment she felt toward herself, Susan ended the pregnancy. When I asked her if she considers this a parenting decision, she resolutely answered that it was. Given the state of her marriage, she knew she wanted to put all of her energy into caring for her son, and she would not be able to do that with a second baby. Since graduating from seminary, Susan had been working full time as a pastor in a congregation, a role that commanded much of her emotional energy as well as her time. "It's difficult to be a mother and a full-time pastor," she said. "It's hard enough with one child. I couldn't imagine how I would do it with two." Sometime after her abortion, and after taking a break from church, she attended a congregation led by a woman pastor whom Susan just adored. One Sunday the minister announced that she was going to have a second child. After the service, Susan went home and wept because she knew that the woman wouldn't return to full-time ministry. She was right.

When Susan had her abortion, it was just days before Holy Week. The residual bleeding was a constant reminder of what happened, a truth that she had to keep to herself at church. Because of the timing of her procedure during a busy season at work, Susan felt she needed to tell her two pastoral colleagues about the abortion. She described their reactions as "not unsupportive or overly supportive." This filled Susan with anger, that she'd been met with such a nonchalant response from her pastoral colleagues when she was struggling with so many things. She needed their support, not their ambivalence. The fact was that she *wanted* to have another child, but because of the dysfunction at home and the demands of her job, she felt like she couldn't.

As time went on, she began to resent church and the need to conceal this part of her life. She was frustrated and confused because what she needed was support in navigating tough questions about her future. Her marriage was becoming more and more toxic, and she didn't know how to extricate herself from the relationship. She knew her family would be devastated, but she also knew she had to choose herself. When her son was five years old, Susan finally left the marriage and started a new chapter of her life as a single mom, which was full of challenges, not the least of which were her financial struggles raising a kid on her own in an expensive city. In the midst of all of this, she had no capacity to process her abortion.

Years later, Susan was invited to do an interview for *Parents* magazine about her abortion, the piece I had read before we met. She felt like this was a way to begin telling her story publicly from the angle of someone who had an abortion while married and pastoring a congregation. After the piece was published, Susan teamed up with her friend and colleague Aspen Baker, with whom she had cofounded the organization Exhale, about a preaching tour to talk about her abortion and all of the experiences we have of feeling like there is no space within our sacred communities to share our deepest struggles. Telling her story, she thought, would be a wake-up call to Christians that one of the reasons the church is in decline is because we aren't talking about the full realities of our lives. What Susan didn't expect was how much connection and community it would bring to her life. By talking about the most difficult parts of her life—her divorce, toxic marriage, struggles with church, abortion—she actually drew people in who wanted to share their stories with her.

What Susan has realized in all of her conversations with people and in reflecting on her own experience is that abortion brings up a lot of early trauma. Some choose to put all of it on the abortion experience itself, but the reality is usually a lot more complicated and goes back to childhood: "I think the messages we get as children about being 'bad,' or being too much, or wanting something we can't have come back when we experience something like abortion—or other struggles like addiction or incarceration. We put ourselves in the category of being 'bad people' who are beyond redemption and who are forever isolated from God and community. But it's not true. We have to figure out a way to tell a different version of the story." When Susan sees pro-life signs, she wonders why their movement doesn't want *her* to have a life: "Why would God want for my life to be over because I had an abortion? We all need community and people to show up for us when things don't go the way we planned or when life isn't pretty. It's not just abortion; it's divorce, abuse, and all the hurts that need healing."

Susan realizes that not everyone is going to be able to tell their abortion stories, but she hopes that by sharing hers, those with hidden stories will feel like theirs have been heard. Sometimes people reach out about their own abortion experiences, asking her how she managed to get through it all. "What did you do to get over this?" they ask. "When am I going to feel better?" She doesn't have an easy answer. She only has her experience. What she does tell them is that it's important that they are asking the questions, and when they are ready, they will find the right people to help them work through them. "Not everyone is going to come out the way I did," Susan said. "But the possibility of goodness, healing, community, and connectedness is far greater when we tell our stories than when we don't."

Rev. Kaeley McEvoy, Washington, DC

last night I was lonely
so i decided i would cry
for my departed child
nine months old
in three days

—excerpt from the poem "Last Night I Was Lonely"

by Kaeley McEvoy

Kaeley was having dinner at the home of her ministry mentor. They were in the midst of a weekend brimming with celebration activities that she'd been helping to plan for months, yet she didn't feel excited or happy. She was tired and sad and wondered how she was going to make it through the rest of the schedule. "What month did you get pregnant?" her mentor asked. "September," Kaeley answered. Silently they counted together on their fingers, the realization hitting them both at the same time. "You know, we could've had a baby at this dinner, and it would have been OK," her minister said. "But I wouldn't have wanted that," Kaeley said.

Nine months before that dinner, Kaeley started her second year at Union Theological Seminary in New York City. She'd entered seminary with energy and excitement, but now she was struggling to engage fully in her studies and ministry internship. She had bouts of depression that left her lethargic, diminished her appetite, and disrupted her thoughts. After two months of feeling this way, her partner asked her when her last period had been. Admittedly, it had been a while. Up until recently, she'd had a long-term contraceptive in her arm, which could account for her late period.

After several positive at-home pregnancy tests, Kaeley and her partner went to the health center at Columbia University to confirm it with a blood test. Afterward they walked to St. John the Divine, a beautiful Episcopal cathedral popular with tourists. Kaeley stepped into one of the side chapels to get some space. Standing there was a four-foot-tall bronze statue called *Christa*, a female depiction of the crucifixion, and she felt reassured that Christ was with her. After praying together, her partner stood outside the chapel door while she called doctor's offices to schedule an abortion. At one point, a tour guide wanted to enter the chapel with a group, but her partner stood guard. "This is a holy place," her partner told the group. "Something holy is happening, and you can't come in here right now."

Navigating the health care system was confusing and difficult. Many doctors Kaeley contacted didn't provide abortion. In fact, fewer than 10 percent of ob/gyns in private practice provide abortion care, and more than a third do not even provide abortion referrals for their patients. Some object on moral or ethical grounds, while others say that they do not know any providers to whom they could make a referral.[2] Many medical schools do not require training or even provide voluntary information about abortion care to their students.[3]

After making dozens of calls, Kaeley finally reached an office where she could schedule an appointment for that same week. The timing of her procedure was fortuitous in that she only had a few weeks until the end of the semester. After a month recovering at home, she was scheduled to travel with a group of classmates to Ecuador for a January-term class on ecofeminism. She was nervous about the trip and questioned whether she was in the right state of mind to go.

At the airport before boarding her flight, she emailed her ministry mentor, disclosed her abortion, and commented, "I guess this explains why I was having so much trouble at work." Kaeley was doing her ministry internship at Judson Memorial Church, a United Church of Christ and Baptist congregation and the birthplace of the Clergy Consultation Service (CCS), the faith-led abortion referral network I described earlier in the book.

While in Ecuador, her class visited a shelter that provided housing and support to women who were survivors of domestic violence. While touring a large garden on the property, the woman who ran the center pointed to a certain bush and said, "This plant can give a woman an abortion." Kaeley began to cry as she thought to herself, *I wish a plant could have given me an abortion.*

Slowly over time, Kaeley began coming back to herself. Her healing came in the most unexpected of places. During chapel services at her seminary, she would offer to watch a classmate's baby, which she found strangely comforting. Once, at a particularly tough moment, Kaeley was crying in the bathroom in between classes when a visitor to seminary approached her to ask, "Do you mind me asking why you are crying?" Kaeley found herself telling this stranger the whole saga: her abortion, her mental health challenges, her confusion about why she was in seminary at all. The woman said to her, "Your baby chose to stay in heaven and not come to earth yet. It wasn't their time. They made that decision." This shift in perspective left Kaeley speechless. She reflected, "I had been so indoctrinated in the idea that it was *my* choice." But now she could see it from a new perspective. A wise stranger had blessed her with a new theological perspective of how souls come to earth. Perhaps this possibility was never meant to be, and that realization helped her let go of what might have been.

Kaeley is now an ordained minister in the United Church of Christ, and currently she serves a congregation in Washington, DC. She wants to share her abortion experience with her community at the right time and in the right context. Even though it still feels raw in some ways, she finds strength and pride in her story. She knows that talking about her abortion as a clergyperson is important because she is committed to preaching and teaching an incarnational theology that affirms the body as sacred and good: "My abortion will always be an experience that puts me in my body, and for that I am grateful."

Afua Ofosu-Barko, Washington, DC

> "I've found so much peace, love, and healing in being part of a church community, and I wouldn't have found that if I hadn't had my abortion. It was a traumatic experience in so many ways, but I was so blessed through it."

From the moment we began talking, I felt an instant heart connection with Afua. She beams with a light-filled joy that is contagious, even filtered through a computer screen. That inner joy, I learned, was rooted in her faith in God, whom she learned from an early age was always for her, always blessing her, and always offering her unconditional love. I had no idea that I could have such a joyous conversation about God and abortion, but that's exactly what I experienced in this interview.

Afua was born in Ghana, but when she was two, her family relocated first to Canada for two years and then to the Bahamas. Afua grew up going to church regularly, which she said gave her a solid foundation in knowing the love of God. After eight years in the Bahamas, her family moved again, this time to Puerto Rico, and perhaps because of the language barrier, they stopped attending church. That was when Afua began to see her faith as something that was personal, but she also admits that it was less central during her adolescence and early adulthood. "I knew God was there," she told me. "But I didn't turn to God unless I was in crisis." (I could relate to that.) After graduating high school in Massachusetts, Afua moved to California to attend college, where she began getting involved with peer education around issues of sexuality and reproductive health. "I showed up to college as a virgin, and I could tell from conversations with friends that none of us knew anything about sex," she said. "My father is a doctor, so I decided before I was sexually active, I was going to educate myself about it. I became a sexual health peer resource counselor because I believe that all of us are going to make different choices, and we should all have accurate information so that we can hopefully make healthier decisions." Afua volunteered with Planned Parenthood and identified as pro-choice, but she had internalized the religious messages that abortion was a sin. More than a decade later, when she would face her own unplanned pregnancy, she would have to confront what she believed about God and abortion.

Most people I interviewed said that they never expected to be faced with an unplanned pregnancy, but for Afua, it was nearly beyond belief. Afua's partner was medically sterile—or so they thought. She was thirty-six years old at the time, and despite her training as a sexuality educator, she still had to deal with old messages she'd internalized from the church about pregnancy and abortion. She thought to herself, *Who has an abortion at thirty-six years old?* Afua saw only one option: to continue the pregnancy.

But being pregnant was making Afua terribly depressed and unhappy. "It was so bad I began to wonder if there was something psychologically wrong with me," she said. When she went to her obstetrician for her seven-week ultrasound, the doctor asked Afua, "Are you happy about this pregnancy? You don't have to do this, and if you choose to end your pregnancy, I want to be sure you are going to be safe." She was grateful to have such an honest, nonjudgmental discussion with her doctor, who provided important information not only about her health care but also about her ability to make a different choice other than to parent.

Making a decision about her pregnancy was agonizing. For weeks, Afua cried, unsure of what to do. She felt like she couldn't pray to God about it because *how would God want to be part of any of this?* Again, those internalized messages about abortion were resurfacing, and as she contemplated ending the pregnancy, she felt the guilt, shame, and disbelief cycle through her. "My sister had eleven miscarriages on her path to parenthood," she said. "How was I going to tell her that I got pregnant with a medically sterile man and was now going to have an abortion?" But in the end, she made an appointment for an abortion because everything inside of her was screaming that she didn't want to do this. Her partner had said that while he did not want to parent, he wouldn't feel right leaving Afua alone to raise a child. She couldn't fathom bringing a life into the world when they were not fully loved and wanted.

Even though she was resolute in her decision, she struggled with guilt. The night before her abortion, Afua fell to her knees in prayer and said to God, "If this is a sin, I need you to forgive me because I have to do this." When she woke in the morning, she felt the presence of God in her room. Words can't fully capture it, she said, but it was like she had been "flooded with love and peace." She knew without a doubt that God saw her, loved her, and would remain with her. She went to the hospital for her abortion with a deep, unmovable peace. Afterward she felt complete relief that "this horrible accident was over" and she could move forward with her life.

Her story reminded me of the moment in Genesis when Hagar encounters a divine presence in the wilderness who calls her by name and whom she calls in response "El-Roi," the God who sees. Like Hagar, Afua was deeply moved by how powerfully God showed up for her at a moment she didn't expect. She'd internalized the idea that abortion was a sin and that God must hate it. She recalled, "I felt like God was not supposed to be here, and yet here he is." That abiding divine presence lasted for ten days after her procedure. It changed her entire understanding of God and abortion: "The church says that abortion is a sin, but then God came to me the morning of my abortion with compassion and love. No one is going to tell me that God wasn't there for me."

When we spoke, Afua had just completed the massive undertaking of reading through the entire Bible in a year, and while she is unclear exactly what God thinks about abortion specifically—we discussed how there is nothing about it in Scripture—she knows that God loves us unconditionally and that nothing, not abortion or anything else, separates us from God. She asked me about my own theology as an ordained minister, and I shared that my understanding aligns with hers: that there is much we do not and cannot know about God, but what I do know is that God loves us and journeys with us through all our life experiences, offering us compassion at every turn.

While Afua felt connected to God, she wasn't connected to a faith community at the time of her abortion. A few months later, a friend invited her to attend a service on Palm Sunday, and after that, she went weekly. That summer the church did a series on overcoming and enduring, and she was moved to tears by the stories she heard of how God shows up for people in their suffering. When a pastor reached out to Afua to set up an introductory meeting, she felt that was an opportunity to share her abortion story. While many in that situation might have encountered shock or judgment, what she received was pure love and compassion. The pastor encouraged her to get involved, to join a small group, and when the time was right, to share her abortion story with others.

One Sunday in her small women's group, she decided to tell her story. She was apprehensive, but again, she was met with compassion, empathy, and love, and perhaps even more surprising, someone else in the group was moved to tell her own abortion story for the very first time. She said, "Our healing comes when we can open up about what has happened to us."

Afua recognizes that so many churches have missed the mark when it comes to conversations about abortion and the other tough decisions we make about our lives. What some communities view as black-and-white issues of right and wrong, Afua sees as the gray of complexity and messiness. "Picking and choosing what to focus on in the Bible has done a lot of harm in the world. It's kept people from embracing God because they think God is against them," she commented. "What I know is that God wouldn't judge a woman for making the best decision for her life. When some churches preach that if you make this one decision, you're going to forever be damned for it—that's not how God works, because God is a God of compassion and love."

Rev. Karen Stoffers-Pugh, Chico, California

"We choose how we respond to the holy, even when we're making choices that are hard and might hurt us."

I had just wrapped up what I originally thought was my final interview for this book when I got an email from Rev. Karen Stoffers-Pugh, a United Methodist clergywoman who wanted to share her story with me. I debated whether or not to schedule a conversation with her—I had more interviews than I knew what to do with at the time. But my intuition told me that I needed to speak with her, that she had something important to tell me. I'm thankful I paid attention to that feeling, and I'm even more thankful that Karen was willing to share with me.

When Karen was in her early twenties, she moved from Northern California to Los Angeles, where she met and married her first husband. Looking back, she can see that she jumped into the relationship too soon, but she was young and in love. When she discovered that she was pregnant, she was excited about having a baby and happily shared the good news with her family and friends. But her husband became emotionally abusive. Karen said, "I was naive and had not realized that he was an addict." Her husband was adamant that she terminate the pregnancy. Karen felt she had nowhere to turn. She didn't want to have to tell her family and close friends the truth: that she had chosen to marry someone who turned out to be abusive and who didn't want to have a child with her. She was deeply ashamed and blamed herself. After the abortion, she lied and told them that she'd had a miscarriage. It wasn't until many years later that she shared what really happened.

Twenty years after her abortion, which she had kept secret from everyone, Karen was reading the local newspaper online when she saw an article about an upcoming healing service that would be held at the local Catholic Church for anyone who had lost a child for any reason. When she got to the sanctuary, she was blown away; it was packed with people. The priest who gave the homily said several things that Karen found healing. First, he shared that Catholic teaching no longer upheld the belief that unbaptized children were in limbo, an afterlife state devoid of suffering but also apart from God. Then he finished his homily by saying, "No matter why your child was not born into this world, they returned to the arms of God."

To conclude the service, everyone gathered had the opportunity to light a tea light on the altar at the center of the sanctuary as a way to commemorate their loss. There was also a table with a book in which they could write their child's name. Karen said it was healing to participate among this group of mourners. "So often with our pain, we think it's unique to us because it's so personal. The healing part was to see all of these women stand up to go forward and to be part of this bigger process," Karen shared with me. What she experienced in that Catholic Church was *grace*.

Looking back, Karen is glad that she made the choice to have an abortion, even though it brought emotional and spiritual pain. She knows that if she had continued the pregnancy, it would've been a terrible situation that would have tied her to an abusive partner. "Sometimes I regret that I didn't just walk away from that marriage and go home to my mom," she said. Sadly, Karen was never able to conceive again. As she struggled with infertility, part of her felt like God was punishing her for having an abortion. More than forty years later, there is still pain surrounding her abortion, but there is no more shame.

I asked Karen how this experience has informed her ministry as a pastor. She responded that she has compassion for people who share their sacred stories and creates spaces for others to tell their truth. She mentioned an event just recently when she was volunteering and a young woman approached her for assistance. Soon she began telling Karen her whole life story and even began to cry. The woman was startled by this, surprised that she'd shared so much and cried with a stranger. Karen chuckled, "Well, I'm a pastor. I create sacred spaces so people can tell their stories, whether they're strangers or members of my congregation. It's my superpower."

From time to time, someone will ask me why I continue to stay in the church when the opposition to abortion is so entangled with Christian dogma. How do I reconcile that enormous gap? My answer is that I continue to hold fast to the beauty and the ancient truth of the sacred story: that we were created with goodness, that we are loved by God, and that we are here to love one another in community. In her book *Mary Magdalene Revealed*, Meggan Watterson writes about "the Christianity we haven't tried yet."[4] It's my fierce belief in the possibility of a world guided by compassion and divine love that propels me forward in this work for justice. Together we can embody a radical, collective love that we have not yet tried but that we believe—that we *know*—is within our reach. So many people are longing for it. May it be so.

CONCLUSION

Creating a Culture of Compassion around
Abortion, Grief, and Healing

Listening to and learning from abortion stories creates a pathway for us to develop our individual and collective capacity to offer compassion to one another. Like I said in the introduction, compassion is not pity or even empathy. It is a *process* of regular, intentional action that centers the one in need.

As a former group fitness instructor, I liken it to building physical strength. When a muscle has been underutilized, building it up requires focus, intentional work, proper form, rest, and patience. We can't speed up the process by overworking our bodies. Too much exercise leads to burnout and injury, which are counterproductive to our goal. What we need is commitment to a long-term plan with steps that are achievable and build strength over time. Our plan needs to take into account that we aren't going to show up the exact same way each day—that our energy and motivation are going to wax and wane. That's why we also need encouragement and accountability to keep us focused on our goal.

The same is true when we begin the journey of creating a culture of compassion around abortion. It feels overwhelming! The challenges are daunting, and the transformation we seek will not happen overnight. That's why I've developed an action plan of steps that will help us collectively build stronger compassion "muscles" to equip for the long work ahead.

Get Clear on Where You Are Starting

Each of us will have different responses to the stories in this book—and that's OK. What's important is that we start from a place of self-awareness. Take some time to reflect on how taking in these stories has impacted you. Which ones stood out? What emotions did they evoke in you, and how did that feel in your body?

It's probable that at some point in your reading, you were triggered. Maybe you felt defensive, judgmental, or apathetic. Maybe you experienced sadness or grief. Honor and accept your feelings, no matter what they are, as an authentic response to what you read. If you feel any overwhelming emotion, tend to yourself. Take a walk, journal, call a friend—whatever you need.

Then spend some time exploring the root of that emotional reaction. Did it remind you of something from your own life or the experience of a loved one? What other factors may have played into your response? You may find journaling or talking with a close friend helpful, or you might find clarity through dedicated times of prayer or meditation. Maybe what you need right now is to stop thinking about this book or abortion altogether. Please listen to your inner knowing! Take a break and come back when you feel ready to resume your journey.

Explore Your Beliefs about Abortion with Curiosity and Kindness

No matter where you are starting from, a values clarification exercise can be helpful in being able to articulate your views to others. One helpful resource is the free guide *The Abortion Option: A Values Clarification Guide for Health Care Professionals* created by the National Abortion Federation. Although this guide was developed specifically for health care providers, the questions and reflection exercises are useful for anyone who wants a better understanding of their personal views on abortion.

Another simple way to start this process is to ask yourself a set of questions like these:

- What messages did you hear about family, sexuality, and abortion growing up? Where did they come from—your family, faith community, school, peers? Are any of the values you hold now in conflict with ones you were taught as a child?
- If you were raised in a spiritual or religious tradition, do you hold the same or different beliefs now? What role does

> spirituality play in your daily life? Do any of your personal values conflict with the teachings of your faith?
>
> - Reflect on your romantic and sexual history. How do those experiences, both positive and negative, impact the way you think about abortion?
> - When do you think life begins? What do you think personhood means? When do you think abortion is morally acceptable or not? Why?

It's OK if you don't have an answer to every question. Pay attention to any emotions that come up as you explore these questions. Were there any times that you felt shame or guilt? Take the time to pause and tend to these places with love and kindness. Whenever we become self-critical, we block ourselves from receiving the love and healing we need to grow and evolve. Compassion starts with accepting ourselves, recognizing that as human beings, we all are flawed and make mistakes and that regardless, we are worthy of kindness and gentleness.

You may want to reach out to a trusted friend or faith leader to talk about what you discovered. There might be questions you want to explore more fully. I've included some helpful books and websites in the resources.

Practice Listening to Abortion Stories without Judgment and Name and Address Stigma as It Arises

As Renee Bracey Sherman has said, "Abortion stigma—the shared understanding that abortion is morally wrong and/or socially unacceptable—is pervasive in our society."[1] Abortion stigma isn't reserved only for those who identify as staunchly anti-choice. It shapes us as a collective. That's why many people who are politically pro-choice also assert that they would never have an abortion themselves and why so many people I interviewed never thought that they would need abortion care.

Each of us must look for the ways that stigma impacts our beliefs and values about abortion. If your initial response to an abortion story in this book or elsewhere is judgment, stop to investigate the source of those assumptions. What are your underlying beliefs about people who have abortions and under what circumstances? What would it look like if you suspended your judgment and approached this situation with an open heart and an open mind?

Compassion centers the person in need of support or care. As you learn about different experiences with abortion, practice maintaining a healthy sense of separateness between their experience and your own feelings. One of the greatest spiritual lessons of this work is remembering that each of us is capable of receiving whatever divine guidance we need when we are making decisions about our lives. Remember that what may be best for you might not be the best for someone else in similar circumstances.

Learn to Respond with Compassion to Situations That Bump up against Your Experience, Beliefs, and Values

Our intention is rarely to hurt someone who is struggling or in pain, yet so often we say and do things that cause harm. When faced with someone's grief or difficulty, we tend to react from our own discomfort, fears, and anxieties, and we end up centering our own needs rather than those of the person coming to us for support. Consider a time when you were in pain and someone offered unhelpful advice or platitudes. What did that feel like? What would have been helpful?

As a practice, compassion is not the same as agreement with someone's decision or even full understanding of their situation. Compassion is opening up room for someone else's experience to be held with love and acceptance, regardless of your ability to relate to or identify with it. When the impulse to judge or criticize comes up, see this as an opportunity to strengthen your compassion muscles by shifting your focus back to the person who is sharing with you. Instead of offering advice, ask thoughtful questions and listen for understanding. The goal is not to be right; the goal is to be open.

Practice Discussing Abortion Compassionately with Others

Let's be honest. Many of us aren't even comfortable saying the word *abortion*. The more you talk about it, the more normal it will feel. Speak with a trusted friend or someone in your life you think might be open to an honest, kind conversation.

If you find yourself in a heated debate, know that you can stop the conversation at any time. You may also ask thoughtful questions. Practice compassionate listening with those who disagree with you.

Engage Your Community in Conversation

Just like you started with a personal assessment of where you are starting, get clear on where your community stands. Is abortion something that is discussed? What about sexuality, reproductive loss, and gender equity? Think about the stated and implicit community values and how they operate.

If you feel there is an opening for this work, start by having conversations with others in the community. This is good practice for developing the skill of normalizing abortion by talking about it. Discuss the kinds of rituals, ministries, and programs that your community already offers. How might they overlap?

If your community has never held an event focused on reproductive loss or reproductive freedom, think about an entry point. Activities like sharing circles, a documentary screening, or a book club can be helpful ways to get people thinking. If you are going to host a discussion, make sure to secure a skilled facilitator to help manage any conflict that might arise.

Discern ways that your faith community can offer compassionate care to people who have abortions. If your community is ready to take compassionate action, there are many things you can do to support people who have abortions:

- offering healing rituals for reproductive loss of all kinds
- providing financial assistance to people who need help paying for their abortions
- making meals or creating care packages for people after their abortions[2]

- advocating to expand and ensure abortion access
- speaking out publicly against harmful abortion restrictions
- volunteering with abortion funds and clinic defense teams
- providing spiritual care to people who have abortions, abortion providers, and staff

Get to know the organizations and people in your area who are already engaged in this work, like abortion funds, clinics, and advocacy organizations. Ask how you can partner with them and what support would be most helpful. Aim to collaborate, not re-create what's already in place.

Remember, this is an ongoing process. As we continue to grow in our compassion, we grow in our capacity to hold space for the myriad experiences people have and meet them with love and acceptance. Each time we offer compassion, we move one step closer to being the kind of people God calls us to be.

RECOMMENDED RESOURCES

ORGANIZATIONS

All-Options—all-options pregnancy support (all-options.org)

Catholics for Choice (catholicsforchoice.org)

Exhale—postabortion emotional support (exhaleprovoice.org)

Faith Aloud (faithaloud.org)

Interfaith Voices for Reproductive Justice (iv4rj.org)

National Abortion Federation (prochoice.org)

National Council of Jewish Women (ncjw.org)

National Network of Abortion Funds (abortionfunds.org)

Religious Coalition for Reproductive Choice (rcrc.org)

Shout Your Abortion (shoutyourabortion.com)

SisterReach (sisterreach.org)

SisterSong (sistersong.net)

We Testify (wetestify.org)

BOOKS

*Handbook for a Post-*Roe *America* by Robin Marty

Killing the Black Body: Race, Reproduction, and the Meaning of Liberty by Dorothy Roberts

Reproductive Justice: An Introduction by Loretta Ross

To Offer Compassion: A History of the Clergy Consultation Service on Abortion by Doris Andrea Dirks and Patricia A. Relf

Trust Women: A Progressive Christian Argument for Reproductive Justice by Rebecca Todd Peters

The Turnaway Study: Ten Years, a Thousand Women, and the Consequences of Having—or Being Denied—an Abortion by Diana Greene Foster, PhD

ACKNOWLEDGMENTS

Writing a book during a global pandemic was not something I set out to do, but I am so grateful for the opportunity to birth this project into the world at a time when the need for compassion, both for ourselves and for the collective, is increasingly apparent. I am grateful for the team at Broadleaf Books for supporting this project and for my editor, Lisa Kloskin, who believed in my ability to take on a book about abortion and healing, who trusted and encouraged me when I felt called to shift and tweak the direction, and who calmly offered support, feedback, and guidance at every step of the way.

There are so many people who were thought partners with me throughout the writing process: Rev. Dr. Cari Jackson, Rev. Dr. Rebecca Todd Peters, Ashley Peterson, Elaina Ramsey, Sonja Spoo, Renee Bracey Sherman, Beth Vial, Dr. Ken Doka, Rev. Susan Chorley, Rabbi Danya Ruttenberg, Tatiana Perkins, and many other colleagues and friends who checked in on me and cheered me on through phone calls, texts, emails, and Zoom meetings. I am grateful for my squad!

Most of all I want to thank the storytellers, the brave and fierce people who trusted me with their experiences and who were willing to share both their wounds and their displays of strength in service of our collective healing. I am forever grateful.

NOTES

CHAPTER 2

1. "Resolution on Abortion," SBC, June 1, 1976, https://www.sbc.net/resource-library/resolutions/resolution-on-abortion-3/.
2. Gillian Frank, "The Deep Ties between the Catholic Anti-abortion Movement and Racial Segregation," Jezebel, January 22, 2019, https://theattic.jezebel.com/the-deep-ties-between-the-catholic-anti-abortion-moveme-1831950706.
3. Frank.
4. For a historical overview, read *Killing the Black Body* by Dorothy Roberts.
5. Pam Chamberlain, "Politicized Science: How Anti-abortion Myths Feed the Christian Right Agenda," *Public Eye Magazine* 20, no. 2 (Summer 2006), http://www.publiceye.org/magazine/v20n2/chamberlain_politicized_science.html.
6. Rebecca J. Cook and Simone Cusack, *Gender Stereotyping: Transnational Legal Perspectives* (Philadelphia: University of Pennsylvania Press, 2010), 88.
7. David C. Reardon, "Restoring Hope, Finding Forgiveness: Despair vs. Hope, Part Two," *Post-Abortion Review* 3, no. 4 (Fall 1995), https://afterabortion.org/restoring-hope-finding-forgiveness-2/.
8. "Clinical Training Catalog," Rachel's Vineyard Ministries, 2014, https://www.rachelsvineyard.org/PDF/Course%20Catalogue/2014CourseCatalog.pdf.
9. See Diana Greene Foster, *The Turnaway Study: Ten Years, a Thousand Women, and the Consequences of Having—or Being Denied—an Abortion* (New York: Scribner, 2020).

10. Kenneth J. Doka, *Disenfranchised Grief: Recognizing Hidden Sorrow* (New York: Lexington, 1989), 6.

CHAPTER 3

1. United Methodist Social Principles, "The Nurturing Community: Abortion," 2016 Book of Discipline, Social Principles, ¶161.K, accessed May 7, 2021, https://tinyurl.com/2rxkxf5m.
2. World Health Organization, "Constitution of the World Health Organization," in *World Health Organization: Basic Documents*, 45th ed. (Geneva: World Health Organization, 2005), https://tinyurl.com/ejp6wu69.
3. Krissi Danielsson, "Ectopic Pregnancy Statistics," Verywell Family, updated March 3, 2021, https://www.verywellfamily.com/what-do-statistics-look-like-for-ectopic-pregnancy-2371730.
4. Jessie Balmert, "Where Did This Ohio Lawmaker Get His Ideas about Implanting Ectopic Pregnancies?," *Columbus Dispatch*, December 11, 2019, https://tinyurl.com/twuh5d49.
5. "How Effective Are Condoms?," Planned Parenthood, accessed May 7, 2021, https://www.plannedparenthood.org/learn/birth-control/condom/how-effective-are-condoms.

CHAPTER 4

1. SAMHSA, *Key Substance Use and Mental Health Indicators in the United States: Results from the 2018 National Survey on Drug Use and Health*, SAMHSA, August 2019, https://tinyurl.com/ybh84mdz.
2. R. C. Kessler et al., "Lifetime Prevalence and Age-of-Onset Distributions of Mental Disorders in the World Health Organization's World Mental Health Survey Initiative," *World Psychiatry* 6, no. 3 (2007): 168–76.

3. Kathleen Rowan, Donna D. McAlpine, and Lynn A. Blewett, "Access and Cost Barriers to Mental Health Care, by Insurance Status, 1999–2010," *Health Affairs (Millwood)* 32, no. 10 (2013): 1723–30, https://doi.org/10.1377/hlthaff.2013.0133.

4. Tahmi Perzichilli, "The Historical Roots of Racial Disparities in the Mental Health System," *Counseling Today*, May 7, 2020, https://tinyurl.com/5dnt7hpu.

5. Erica Martin Richards, "Mental Health among African-American Women," John Hopkins Medicine, accessed May 7, 2021, https://tinyurl.com/25ax7ywm.

6. Foster, *Turnaway Study*, 109.

7. Brenda L. Bauman et al., "Vital Signs: Postpartum Depressive Symptoms and Provider Discussions about Perinatal Depression—United States, 2018," *Morbidity and Mortality Weekly Report* 69 (2020): 575–81, http://dx.doi.org/10.15585/mmwr.mm6919a2.

8. Alessandra Biaggi et al., "Identifying the Women at Risk of Antenatal Anxiety and Depression: A Systematic Review," *Journal of Affective Disorders* 191 (February 2016): 62–77, https://doi.org/10.1016/j.jad.2015.11.014.

9. "Fact Sheet: Induced Abortion in the United States," Guttmacher Institute, September 2019, https://www.guttmacher.org/fact-sheet/induced-abortion-united-states.

10. Sarah C. M. Roberts et al., "Risk of Violence from the Man Involved in the Pregnancy after Receiving or Being Denied an Abortion," *BMC Medicine* 12, no. 144 (September 2014), https://bmcmedicine.biomedcentral.com/articles/10.1186/s12916-014-0144-z.

11. The Hyde Amendment prohibits any federal funding from being used for abortion services, except in the cases of incest, rape, or life of the pregnant person. According to the Repeal Hyde Art Project, the bird is "representative of the self-determination, resistance, and resilience of people who confront and overcome barriers to abortion care everyday [*sic*]. It is also a positive

symbol that represents the hope for change." "Why the Bird?,"
Repeal Hyde Art Project, accessed May 7, 2021, https://www
.repealhydeartproject.org/why-the-bird.

12. Jeana Nam, "I Hope the Christian Church Makes Room for Abortion Stories like Mine," Popsugar, March 28, 2020, https://www
.popsugar.com/news/what-it-like-to-have-abortion-when-youre
-christian-47321241.

CHAPTER 5

1. "Abortion and Parental Involvement Laws," Advocates for Youth,
accessed May 7, 2021, https://tinyurl.com/s857tcar.

2. Amanda Jean Stevenson, Kate Coleman-Minahan, and Susan
Hays, "Denials of Judicial Bypass Petitions for Abortion in Texas
before and after the 2016 Bypass Process Change: 2001–2018,"
American Journal of Public Health 110, no. 3 (2020): 351–53, https://
doi.org/10.2105/AJPH.2019.305491.

3. Committee on Adolescence, "The Adolescent's Right to Confidential Care When Considering Abortion," *Pediatrics* 139, no. 2
(February 2017): e20163861, https://pediatrics.aappublications
.org/content/139/2/e20163861.

4. Hafrún Finnbogadóttir and Anna-Karin Dykes, "Increasing Prevalence and Incidence of Domestic Violence during the Pregnancy
and One and a Half Year Postpartum, as Well as Risk Factors: A
Longitudinal Cohort Study in Southern Sweden," *BMC Pregnancy
and Childbirth* 16, no. 327 (2016), https://bmcpregnancychildbirth
.biomedcentral.com/articles/10.1186/s12884-016-1122-6.

5. "Our Whole Lives: Lifespan Sexuality Education," Unitarian Universalist Association, accessed May 7, 2021, https://www.uua.org/
re/owl.

6. Doris Andrea Dirks and Patricia Relf, *To Offer Compassion: A History of the Clergy Consultation Service on Abortion* (Madison: University of Wisconsin Press, 2017), 51.

7. Dirks and Relf, 44.

8. "Abortion Funds 101," National Network of Abortion Funds, accessed May 7, 2021, https://abortionfunds.org/about/abortion -funds-101/.

9. "My Abortion Helped Me Take Control of My Life," Jane's Due Process, September 15, 2019, https://janesdueprocess.org/blog/ my-abortion-helped-me-take-control-of-my-life/.

10. CoWanda Rusk, "I Went to Christian Summer Camp and Left an Abortion Activist," Rewire News Group, May 22, 2020, https:// tinyurl.com/34bdctzx.

11. CoWanda Rusk, "How My Abortion Strengthened My Faith," Blavity, September 11, 2020, https://blavity.com/how-my -abortion-strengthened-my-faith?category1=opinion.

CHAPTER 6

1. "Unintended Pregnancy in the United States," Guttmacher Institute, January 2019, https://www.guttmacher.org/fact-sheet/ unintended-pregnancy-united-states.

2. CDC Reproductive Health, "Pregnancy Mortality Surveil- lance System," CDC, accessed May 7, 2021, https://tinyurl.com/ 2wjyrfkr.

3. Gretchen Livingston, "The Changing Profile of Unmarried Parents," Pew Research Center, April 25, 2018, https://www .pewsocialtrends.org/2018/04/25/the-changing-profile-of -unmarried-parents/.

4. National Center for Health Statistics, "Health Insurance Cover- age," CDC, accessed May 7, 2021, https://www.cdc.gov/nchs/ fastats/health-insurance.htm.

5. Bridget Ansel and Matt Markezich, "Falling behind the Rest of the World: Childcare in the United States," Washington Cen- ter for Equitable Growth, January 25, 2017, https://tinyurl.com/ 8a3kysuy.

6. Elena Gutierrez et al., *Undivided Rights: Women of Color Organizing for Reproductive Justice* (Chicago: Haymarket, 2016).
7. Gutierrez et al., viii.
8. Emilie K. Johnson et al., "Fertility-Related Care for Gender and Sex Diverse Individuals: A Provider Needs-Assessment Survey," *Transgender Health* 1, no. 1 (October 2016): 197–201, https://tinyurl.com/ywh9xpky.
9. Liz Elting, "Why Pregnancy Discrimination Still Matters," *Forbes*, October 30, 2018, https://tinyurl.com/3cc6aku3.
10. Kim Jorgensen Gane, "Kim Jorgensen Gane Reading What If I'd Said 'Just Drive?,'" Listen to Your Mother, July 10, 2014, YouTube video, 5:32, https://www.youtube.com/watch?v=TGzJSBvJuos.

CHAPTER 8

1. Jenna Jerman, Rachel K. Jones, and Tsuyoshi Onda, "Characteristics of U.S. Abortion Patients in 2014 and Changes since 2008," Guttmacher Institute, May 2016, https://www.guttmacher.org/report/characteristics-us-abortion-patients-2014.
2. "Most U.S. Obstetrician-Gynecologists in Private Practice Do Not Provide Abortions and Many Also Fail to Provide Referrals," Guttmacher Institute, November 27, 2017, https://tinyurl.com/paj9vcyz.
3. American College of Obstetricians and Gynecologists, "Abortion Training and Education," *Obstetrics and Gynecology* 124 (2014): 1055–59, https://tinyurl.com/4k3xv9p7.
4. Meggan Watterson, *Mary Magdalene Revealed: The First Apostle, Her Feminist Gospel, and the Christianity We Haven't Tried Yet* (Carlsbad: Hay House, 2019).

CONCLUSION

1. Renee Bracey Sherman and the Sea Change Program, "Executive Summary: Saying Abortion Aloud: Research and Recommendations for Public Abortion Storytellers and Organizations," Renee Bracey Sherman, accessed May 7, 2021, https://tinyurl.com/fmj37u6n.
2. These can be simple: a small bag of things like snacks, tea, pads, supportive literature, notebooks, and so on. For a model of abortion care packages, visit abortioncarepackage.org.